IN THE LIGHT
OF DEATH

This book is dedicated to all those searching

for a love that is big enough

to embrace both joy and sorrow,

and a wisdom that is deep enough

to reach the Mystery.

First published in Great Britain in 2002

by Godsfield Press Ltd

Laurel House, Station Approach, Alresford

Hampshire SO24 9JH, U.K.

www.godsfieldpress.com

2 4 6 8 10 9 7 5 3

Designed for Godsfield Press by The Bridgewater Book Company

Printed and bound in China

ISBN 1–84181–169–6

CONTENTS

INTRODUCTION

Death is not the extinguishing of the light,
but the blowing out of the candle because
the dawn has come.

Rabindranath Tagore
Indian Sage

DEATH AND SPIRITUALITY

Being with the dying and bereaved is the most humbling experience I know.
There are no easy answers to offer someone who faces the greatest of fears and the
most agonizing of losses. Writing this book has been a profound challenge
because, before the enormity of death and grief, words are not sufficient. Yet in
a book words are all we have, so we must use words to reach beyond words and
awaken something deeper: genuine love and authentic wisdom.

The philosophical insights, practical guided meditations, and personal
anecdotes that make up this little book draw on my experience as a bereavement
counselor, and as a facilitator of residential retreats on spirituality and death. This
work gave me the privilege of sharing with complete strangers moments of intimate
vulnerability, naked reality, bittersweet poignancy, deep connection, overwhelming
compassion and transcendent wonder. It showed me beyond doubt that it is often
during the times of our greatest confusion and suffering that we have the greatest
opportunity to grow. It convinced me that death is a powerful teacher that, through
pain and suffering, challenges us to discover who we really are, shows us what
really matters, and leads us to a deep love that embraces both joy and sorrow.

When I began working with the dying and bereaved, death was a taboo subject. Since that time things have begun to change. There has been a plethora of publications designed to help us cope with dying and recover from loss. But this is not one of those books. *In the Light of Death* explores the spiritual perspective on death and loss, but it does more than offer advice and comfort to help us cope and recover. Spiritual philosophy seeks to transform our understanding of death completely. It boldly suggests that death is not an horrendous evil at all, but rather an integral part of existence, to be embraced and not feared. It offers a completely positive approach to life and death in which dying, aging, suffering, and grief are portrayed as parts of a process of spiritual awakening. Of becoming aware of a love so deep it mitigates all our heartache and misery. Of realizing we are more than we can possibly imagine. Of discovering a profound faith, beyond the scope of words to ever express, that everything is fine. Things are meant to be the way they are. Life is good and death is safe.

The spiritual philosophy that informs this book is sometimes called the perennial philosophy, because it is a universally human wisdom taught by saints and sages from all times and all cultures. The perennial philosophy teaches that we fear death because we mistakenly believe ourselves to be a physical body. The spiritual path is the process of dispelling this illusion and becoming aware of our deeper immortal nature. The death of the body is the supreme opportunity to realize our true identity and in so doing fulfill the very purpose of our existence. Life is a journey of spiritual awakening and death is the final challenge.

For the saints and sages, living with an awareness of death is not life-denying but life-enhancing. In my experience, they are right. In the face of death all my worries and ambitions seem inconsequential. My achievements, or lack of them, become irrelevant. The silly melodramas of my day-to-day life, which would otherwise threaten to consume me, become amusing and ridiculous. Somehow, I know that all that really matters is the simple love

I share with others, and the appreciation of the gift of life, with all its joys and woes. Contemplating death wakes me up to the wonder of living. As you read this book, I hope that you will also find this to be true.

Let's take an overview of the journey we will be making.

In Chapter 1, *Fear and Denial*, we will face our fear of death.

In Chapter 2, *In the World but Not of It*, we will explore the simple secret at the heart of the perennial philosophy, which turns our commonsense ideas about who we are inside out and reveals our true immortal identity.

In Chapter 3, *The Afterlife and Reincarnation*, we will investigate the Near-Death Experience and what the saints and sages tell us about life after death.

In Chapter 4, *Old Age and Illness*, we will look at the spiritual perspective on aging and suffering.

In Chapter 5, *Love and Loss*, we will examine bereavement and how to love and let go.

In Chapter 6, *Big Mind*, we will attempt to understand the essence of the perennial philosophy that underlies and informs all of these teachings.

The perennial philosophy is not just another interesting theory about life and death. It is an attempt by the saints and sages to describe their immediate experience of the way things really are. Their teachings are designed to help us to see this for ourselves. To assist this process, there are guided meditations at the end of each chapter. You can read these meditations through and then perform them from memory, but it may be better to read them onto a tape to which you can subsequently listen. Or better still, work with a spiritual friend and read them to each other. Practicing these meditations with a friend can be very helpful because you can discuss your reactions together afterward. Don't hurry these exercises. Be prepared to return to some practices many times. Usually the more time you give to them, the more rewarding they are.

I do not know why you are reading this. Perhaps you are facing your own imminent death or recent loss? Perhaps you are responding to a deep spiritual need to explore your mortality? Whatever your situation, I offer this little book to you with humility and respect. I do not presume to know what you're going through. I do not have easy answers for impossible problems. From a sense of our shared vulnerability as human beings I pass on to you what I have learned from others, in the hope that you may find something of value on your unique life-journey. It is your life that has led you to this moment. It is your courage that has inspired you to pick up a book on a subject that most people would prefer to avoid. It will be your revelations that bring you peace and faith in the face of death.

FEAR AND DENIAL

This life of ours is as transient as autumn clouds.
To watch the birth and death of all beings
is like looking at the movements of a dance.
A lifetime is a flash of lightning in the sky.
It rushes by like a torrent down a steep slope.

The Buddha
Indian sage

An event of incomparable importance awaits you. This moment, compared to which all the dramas of your life pale into insignificance, is an inevitability you can neither predict nor avoid. You do not know when it will happen or how it will happen, but happen it will. And not just to you, but to me also. Indeed, to all of us at different times and in different ways.

You'd think that the existence of such a mysterious fate would dominate our thoughts and be a constant source of conversation and speculation. Yet this extraordinary event is, strangely, ignored. More than ignored, it is avoided. This mystery is so big it scares us into silence. So final it frightens us frozen. So far beyond our everyday experience that most of us choose to live without acknowledging it at all. That is until circumstances outside our control force us to stop pretending to ourselves and face the awesome truth. Life ends in death.

To bring our attention to this, the ultimate cover-up, a satirical artist friend of mine once produced a spoof newspaper banner that announced:

SHOCKING NEWS

BILLIONS FACE DEATH!

His exposé pointed out the startling fact that within little more than a hundred years everyone now alive would be dead! Obvious, of course, when you think about it. But that's just what most of us try not to do—think about it. As the Buddhist sage Milarepa puts it:

Strong and healthy,
who thinks of sickness,
until it strikes like lightning?

Preoccupied with the world,
who thinks of death,
until it arrives like thunder?

More than a quarter of a million people die every day. Stop and imagine that for a moment. All that fear and suffering and loss and release and revelation—happening right now. Whether you come to this book as someone curious about death, or facing your own imminent death, or grieving for the loss of a loved one, make no mistake about it, you are not alone. We face death together. It is the human condition.

Death is not an optional experience. Your mother bequeathed you your death when she gave you your birth. From your first breath your last breath is inevitable. Every year most of us celebrate our birthday. It is unsettling to think that each year we also pass by an anonymous date that will become our deathday. Although we assume tomorrow will always come, one day it won't. And the day that is our last may be today. Statistically we may know approximately how many people will die each day, but we don't know who. It could be me. It could be you. It could be one of those we love so dearly.

Is it morbid and depressing to think such thoughts? The answer from contemporary culture is "yes." Although over the last few decades attitudes have begun to change, death remains a taboo subject to be politely sidestepped or dismissed quickly with glib platitudes and a grim smile. It is something, quite simply, we wish didn't exist. Our health professionals treat death as a failure of modern medicine to keep us alive. Bereavement is regarded as if it were an unfortunate psychological condition from which we need to recover, or an annoying impediment to ordinary life with which we must learn to cope. We encourage the old to be obsessed by youth. We tell the terminally ill that they will be better soon. Better a sweet lie than the bitter truth. After all, life must go on.

Why are we so frightened of death? That sounds like a stupid question, because the answer seems so obvious. We don't know what death is and fear it may be the perpetual darkness. What we do know about death we don't like. It takes away from us our loved ones. It ridicules our dreams and aspirations. It robs us of our wealth and achievements. It is something we are hardwired in our biological makeup to resist and prevent at all costs.

Yet not everyone treats death as the enemy. Since the most ancient of times there have been many extraordinary men and women for whom death is a friend. A great teacher, not a thief. A revealer of the truth, who challenges us to discover that our true identity is not the mortal body, which will undoubtedly turn back into the dust from which it came. The legendary Egyptian sage Hermes Trismegistus teaches:

Most people are ignorant of the Truth and therefore afraid of death, believing it to be the greatest of all evils. But death is only the dissolution of a worn-out body.

For the saints and sages, death is the revelation that we are not the limited physical form we usually take ourselves to be, but something greater and more glorious. Death is transformation, not extinction. Death is a new beginning as well as an end. Death is not the perpetual darkness, but a glimpse of eternal splendor. Death is not meaningless, it is the fulfillment of life. As the Sufi sage Rumi writes:

I have often heard it said
"Life would be great if it didn't end in death."
What nonsense!
Without death life is meaningless. Like a harvest left to rot.

SCIENCE, RELIGION, SPIRITUALITY

All religions teach that death is not the end. In our skeptical age, however, we have rightly learned to treat such optimism with caution, even disdain. The great scientific achievements of modernity have come only through questioning the dogmatic assertions of religion. Most human beings throughout history may have believed in life after death, but that doesn't mean they were right. Truth is not democratic. The vast majority of people throughout history also believed the world to be flat, but it turned out to be a sphere hurtling through space.

According to polls, even today in our increasingly scientific Western culture, the majority continue to believe in life after death. Is this some deep intuition or simply wishful thinking? For many scientists it is the last vestige of our superstitious past to which we cling in order to mitigate our fear.

We seem to be faced with the choice of either the dubious reassurance of religious blind faith or cold, clinical, scientific materialism, which dares to debunk our comfortable assumptions and reveal the real, no matter how disquieting. Faced with this stark dichotomy, no wonder so many of us choose not to choose, and avoid thinking about death at all. But the alternatives of religious belief or scientific skepticism obscure another option: the spiritual perspective as articulated by the perennial philosophy.

For historical reasons, we tend to think of spirituality and religion as fundamentally the same thing, but I would like to suggest that they are actually quite different. Many people find spirituality through the traditions and rituals of religion, and I do not want to disparage this in any way. But I do want to clearly distinguish the extremes of mystical spirituality and fundamentalist religion, to help those who have rejected religion to realize that they do not also need to reject spirituality, and so "throw the baby out with the bath water," as it were.

Fundamentalist religion trades in unsubstantiated assertions about what life is, who we are, and how to view death. Mystical spirituality, on the other hand, is akin to science in that it encourages us to question all our assumptions. Fundamentalist religion is about accepting tradition. Mystical spirituality requires us to break through the boundaries of our cultural conditioning and see life in new ways, by examining reality for ourselves. Religion presents us with a set of doctrines to be believed. Spirituality offers an intellectual framework to facilitate a process of spiritual awakening that leads to a direct apprehension of the Truth.

A comment of a participant in one of the retreats I facilitated captured the experience of spiritual awakening completely. She arrived a somber young woman, dressed from head to toe in black, very cut off within herself, with a cynical attitude stemming from years of hurt. Through the vulnerability, warmth, and wisdom of all the participants in the event, she gradually melted. She emerged at the end smiling, soft, open, and so full of love it was pouring out of her. When I asked for comments on how the retreat had affected everyone, she thought to herself, trying to find the right words, and eventually quietly announced "I feel like a convert to…something." That's it exactly.

When you get the message of the mystics you become a convert to "something." Something wonderfully liberating, yet so mysterious you can never quite define it. Something so elusive you can never hold on to it, but must rediscover it in every moment. There is no cult to join or doctrine to proselytize. You have simply joined the ranks of mystical explorers who recognized life to be a natural process of spiritual awakening.

Spiritual awakening brings a confidence in the fundamental goodness of life and death, which transcends belief. A faith, not in theories, but born of direct acquaintance with the secret Source of All, which different spiritual traditions call God, Tao, Allah, Brahmin, the Self, or simply the Great Mystery. Only this, say the saints and sages, can truly sustain us in the face of death.

The blind belief in dogma encouraged by religion may claim to offer solace but actually tends to engender superstitious fear. Every week I pass a lone figure preaching in the streets of the small town in England where I live. He shouts loudly (while thankfully no one listens!), hoping to offer salvation to the lost. But he is oblivious to the terrible message he is actually promoting. "WHERE WILL YOU SPEND ETERNITY? IN HEAVEN OR HELL?" proclaims the board by his side. This is not spiritual reassurance of the essential goodness of life and death. It is religious intimidation to sign up to his particular religious cult or face the consequences— and in this case that means being tortured forever by a God of love! This has nothing to do with spirituality.

Religion claims to bring us together, but it usually ends up dividing us into the "ins" and the "outs." I remember the poignant sadness of attending the funeral of a young friend of mine who died of AIDS. He had been born the homosexual son of Fundamentalist Christian parents, a terrible dilemma with which I witnessed him bravely wrestle for years. And here, at his funeral, that dilemma was graphically laid out for all to see.

On one side of the congregation sat his gay lover and friends, a motley crew of Bohemian misfits of which I was one. On the other side sat his Christian family and their friends. We all loved S—that is why we were there. Yet, while his free-thinking friends remembered S with great respect and affection, his family sat, with the supposed comfort of dogmatic certainty, convinced that S had incurred the just wrath of God for his unclean homosexual activities and that he must now pay the price for those activities in the afterlife. I cannot think of a bleaker and less spiritual perspective.

Religion offers an unquestionable creed. Spirituality on the other hands offers us radical doubt. And this is something far more valuable, because only doubt leads to genuine certainty, while blind belief leads no further than itself. If we can distinguish mystical spirituality from fundamentalist religion we can reject religion without abandoning spirituality. We will then have an intelligent alternative to the soul-destroying scientific materialism that is becoming increasingly fashionable in the modern world.

For those seduced by the wonderful achievements of science into the belief that it has all the answers, however, the spiritual approach can still seem to be a refusal to face facts. There is now a growing faith that science has shown that matter is all there is and that anything spiritual is airy-fairy nonsense. From this perspective, human beings are simply physical bodies, thrown up by accident through an arbitrary process of evolution, who will live out their short lives and then cease to be. But is this materialism actually what science shows us or is this simply a new form of doctrinaire fundamentalism?

Although it is often assumed that all scientists are materialists, nothing could be farther from the truth. Scientific materialists claim that ultimately everything can be reduced to physics—the study of physical matter. Yet the great physicists themselves have not been materialists at all. If you check out any of the influential physicists of the twentieth century, such as Schroedinger, Heisenberg, Pauli, de Broglie, Jeans, Planck, Eddington, Bohr, and Einstein, you may be surprised to find that they are all self-proclaimed Platonic mystics! Their view was that the existential mysteries of life and death are outside the remit of science, and require a different form of investigation.

This is what the perennial philosophy offers. We do not, therefore, have to reject science to embrace spirituality, or reject spirituality to embrace science. Following the example of these great physicists, we can understand empirical science and mystical spirituality as complementary ways of exploring who we are and what life is all about.

FACING OUR FEAR

If we are no more than a physical body that will one day turn to dust, as materialists teach, then it is perfectly rational to fear death, and the best way to be happy is probably not to think about it. Spirituality, however, suggests that we are much more than a physical body and that death is not something to be feared or to be escaped from through denial. It is the supreme challenge toward which our life is leading. The Pagan philosopher Plato teaches: "The best life is spent preparing for death." Most of us, however, find the thought of death so frightening that we push it to the back of the mind, where it turns into a perpetual source of unconscious, debilitating anxiety. When we see death for what it is, however, it is not so terrifying. It is our fear that is the problem, rather than death. The Pagan philosopher Epictetus teaches:

It is your fear of death that terrifies you. You can think about a thing in many ways. Scrutinize your idea of death. Is it true? Is it helpful? Don't fear death. Rather, fear your fear of death.

The Sufi sage Attar teaches: "The only cure for our fear of death is to look death constantly in the face." To overcome our fear we need to look at what we fear, by being aware that each day may be our deathday and each interaction with a loved one our last goodbye. Islamic scripture urges:

In the evening do not expect to live till morning, and in the morning do not expect to live until evening. Prepare as long as you are in good health for sickness, and so long as you are alive for death.

When we ignore our fear it festers, but when we face our fear it gradually diminishes. I remember a girl who attended a group I ran for bereaved young people relating how she liked to watch horror movies on video. When she reached a part she found terrifying she would rewind the video and watch this extract again and again, until she was no longer frightened. I was able to suggest that, in the same way, by going over and over the death of her mother and the fear it had engendered, she would eventually come to peace, which she gradually did.

Fear finally dissipates through familiarity. We fear what we imagine death to be. If we face our fear, the saints and sages assure us, we will find that death is a friend, not a foe. A teacher, not an adversary. On his deathbed the mystic and Beat poet Allen Ginsberg enthused, "I thought I would be terrified, but actually I feel exhilarated."

MEDITATION 1

Unexpected Illness

Many spiritual traditions offer seekers the chance to confront and overcome their fear by going through a form of ritual death. Initiates of the ancient Pagan Mystery religion, for example, were buried in a great trench leaving only the head exposed. These initiations often took place at midnight and would have been terrifying experiences. The Native Americans have a practice called the "Night of Fear" in which seekers go out into the wilderness alone and dig a shallow grave in which they lie throughout the night. Without food or water, exposed to the elements, surrounded by the menacing darkness, lonely and filled with doubt, they face their deepest fears. The following meditation exercises are less dramatic ways of getting us in touch with the reality of our own death.

I remember at one of my retreats a remarkable man who was dying of cancer commenting to the rest of the group, none of whom were terminally ill, "This is just a game to you, but to me this is a reality." At first it was hard to hear this, but actually it helped us all treat the meditations more seriously. These exercises are, of course, a type of game. But what they are trying to put us in touch with is not. If you come to this book as someone who is terminally ill or recently bereaved you may well not need these exercises, or find them simply too graphic in your exposed condition. For the rest of us, however, they can help bring home the fact of our mortality. Only truly acknowledging this can evoke the intense need to know, which will make our spiritual search authentic and sincere.

Preparation
- Sit quietly in a position you find comfortable. Be relaxed but alert.
- Close your eyes and rest your attention on your breath as it comes and goes.
- Let your breath settle into a slow and regular pattern as you let go of all agitation.

Meditation
- Imagine that you have been diagnosed as terminally ill, with only a few months left to live.
- What are your feelings and thoughts?
- What do you want to do with the time you have left?
- How will you sustain yourself through the difficult days ahead?
- Who will you turn to for help and support?
- What is your greatest fear?
- What is your greatest hope?
- What sort of funeral would you like and why?
- How would you like to be remembered?
- When you are ready open your eyes and write down all your thoughts and feelings so that you can contemplate them, now and at some later date.

MEDITATION 2

Buddhist Meditation on a Decaying Corpse

This meditation exercise is a Buddhist practice in which we imagine ourselves to be a decaying corpse. This is not for the fainthearted, but it is a powerful method for confronting our bodily mortality. Leave plenty of time between each stage.

Preparation

- Lie down quietly with your hands by your side and completely relax in a dark room or with only the light of a candle.
- Close your eyes and rest your attention on your breath as it comes and goes. Let your breath settle into a slow and regular pattern as you let go of all agitation.

Meditation

- Imagine that you are about to die.
- Let out a long last breath.
- Imagine that you are a corpse growing slowly colder.
- Imagine that the corpse is now cold and rigid.
- Imagine that the corpse is turning blue.
- Imagine cracks appearing in the skin.
- Imagine parts of the body are beginning to decompose.
- Imagine that the whole body is decomposing.
- Imagine that the corpse is now a skeleton with odd pieces of decaying flesh still adhering to it.
- Imagine that all that now remains is a pile of bones.
- Imagine that the bones are reduced to a handful of dust.
- Imagine that the dust is blown away by the wind leaving nothing at all.
- Who are "you" now?
- When you are ready, open your eyes.

IN THE WORLD BUT NOT OF IT

What lesson have we learned from those who best understand the human condition? Surely, that you must not think of me as this person who can be touched and grasped by the senses. My true Self is remote from the body, without color and without shape, not to be touched by human hands.

Porphyry
Pagan philosopher

Our fear of death is rooted in the conviction that we are a physical body that was born and that one day will die. The perennial philosophy, however, challenges this commonsense assumption and offers a radically different view of who we really are, which quite literally turns the world inside out. In this chapter we will explore this extraordinary vision. These teachings may well seem strange and incomprehensible, as they once did to me, but it is worth persevering. (It is, after all, a matter of life and death!) Although the spiritual vision of your true identity is elusive and subtle, when you get it, you may be surprised at how obvious it actually is. You may find yourself laughing out loud in amazement, as I did, that you missed it for so long.

The message of the mystics is this. Don't just accept the views of others. Look within and examine your own nature for yourself. If you do, you will discover that you are not the physical body you take yourself to be. Rather, your true identity is what Buddhists call "Buddha-nature," Hindus call "Atman," and Christians call "Spirit"—all of which signify what we today call "Consciousness."

The saints and sages want to flip your commonsense view of who you are right around. You presume yourself to be a conscious body, but actually you are Consciousness that is conscious of a body. You are the witness of all you think, feel, and sense. You are an experiencer of experiences. You are Consciousness. This is the simple secret at the heart of the perennial philosophy.

What does it mean to be Consciousness? To describe Consciousness the saints and sages often use terms such as "emptiness" or "the void" or "spaciousness." Although to begin with I found this very confusing, it gave me the clue I needed to get the vision. One day I simply stopped presuming myself to be a body in the world and instead imagined myself as a vast emptiness that embraced everything that I experience. A mysterious presence within which all that exists for me has its existence.

As I examined my experience, I realized that I knew about my physical body and the world through sensation—seeing, hearing, smelling, tasting, and touching. I remember a flash of insight as something remarkable dawned on me. Sensations are experiences in Consciousness. My physical body and the world exist in *me* in the form of sensations. I am not a body in the world. I am the emptiness of Consciousness that *contains* the body and the world!

UNBORN AND UNDYING

In The Gospel of Thomas, a Gnostic Christian text, Jesus promises:

I will reveal to you what no eye can see, what no ear can hear, what no hand can touch, what cannot be conceived by the human mind.

What is it that cannot be seen, heard, touched, or imagined? It is that which does the seeing, hearing, touching, and imagining. The revelation to which the saints and sages wish to lead you is that your true nature is Consciousness.

If you understand this, Jesus promises, you "will not taste death." This is because when you realize you are Consciousness, you know that you are not the mortal body. Rather, you are that which witnessed the body being born and which will one day witness it die. This is the discovery of what the Gnostic Christians call your essential "unbornness." *You* can't possibly die because *you* were never born!

The Hindu guru Ramana Maharshi explains:

If you think that you were born you cannot avoid the fear of death. Examine whether your true Self has actually been born. You will discover that the Self always exists and that the body which is born resolves itself into thought, and that the emergence of thought is the root of all your problems. Discover that from which thoughts emerge. Then you will be able to abide in the ever-present inmost Self and be free from the idea of birth or the fear of death.

The message of the mystics is this. You temporarily appear to be a body that exists in time and that will one day run out of time, but your true Self exists outside time altogether. You are eternal Consciousness that witnesses the world of time. The body is mortal and ever-changing, but you are immortal and never-changing. You are the emptiness of pure awareness. Unborn and undying

Consciousness. The Tibetan lama Sogyal Rinpoche explains: "The essential nature of mind is the background to the whole of life and death, like the sky, which folds the universe in its embrace."

I remember, several years ago, suddenly *getting* what the saints and sages are saying, while reading the following passage from a talk by the Hindu guru Sri Nisargadatta Maharaj. He teaches:

You have squeezed yourself into the span of a lifetime and the volume of a body, and thus created the innumerable conflicts of life and death. Have your being outside this body of birth and death, and all your problems will be solved. They exist because you believe yourself born to die. Undeceive yourself and be free. You are not a person.

The words "You are not a person" jumped out of the page at me. What an audacious and confronting thing to say! I found myself repeating in amazement "I am not a person…I am not a person." And as I did so the truth of this astonishing statement became apparent. I was the vast emptiness of Consciousness that believed itself to be a tiny physical form. I was not a body in the world. The world and the body existed in me. The shock sent me into spasms of uncontrollable, hysterical laughter. It was just so funny. All this time I had unconsciously made one very basic assumption about who I was. I presumed I was a person. When I asked "Who am I?" I was seeking to discover what sort of person I was. Now I could clearly see, beyond doubt, that I was not a person at all, and that this ridiculous assumption was the root of all my problems. Especially my fear of death.

Having let go of the "I am the body" idea, I could see that my true identity was actually obvious from my daily experience of waking and dreaming. From the outside I appear to be a body that is sometimes awake and sometimes asleep.

But when I examined my own experience, I realized that this is not how it is for me at all. In the waking state I appear to be a body in the world. When I go to sleep, however, my body and the world completely disappear and I appear to be a different person living in some other dreamworld. The body comes and goes within Consciousness, which is my true identity. To others I appear to be a body that is sometimes conscious. But when I examine who I am for myself, I see that I am Consciousness that is sometimes conscious of the physical body. Why should I fear death when I already experience, each day, the body coming and going within Consciousness?

The essence of the extraordinary teachings of the perennial philosophy is this. The body was born in you and will die in you. It is a passing appearance within Consciousness. Your fear of death arises because you mistakenly believe yourself to be a physical body. The spiritual path of overcoming the fear of death and discovering your immortality could not be easier. Simply "look within" and examine what you really are for yourself. The *Katha Upanishad*, a Hindu scripture, teaches:

God made the senses turn outwards, man therefore looks outwards, not into himself. Now and again a daring soul, desiring immortality, has looked back and found himself. He who knows the soundless, odorless, tasteless, intangible, formless, deathless, supernatural, undecaying, beginningless, endless, unchangeable Reality, springs out of the mouth of death.

THE DREAM OF LIFE

From the spiritual perspective the paradox of our predicament is that "We are in the world but not of it," as Jesus puts it. We appear to be a physical body in the world, but essentially we exist outside of the world altogether, beyond both life and death. To elucidate these teachings the saints and sages often compare life to a dream. I find this helpful because I can easily see how, although I often appear as a character in my dreams, the whole dream exists within me as Consciousness. In the same way, I can then see that the waking world is an experience within me as Consciousness, just like a dream. Although I appear to be a character in the dream, I am actually the dreamer.

The mystics teach that at death we will wake from the dream of life, but this is no more tragic than when we suddenly wake in the middle of a dream at night. The Taoist sage Chuang Tzu teaches:

To desire life and fear death is crazy. This world is only a passing dream which the sleeper is convinced is real, until unexpectedly the dawn of death frees him from this fantasy. Some who wake from a good dream are upset, whilst others who wake from a bad dream are pleased. Death is the great awakening, but few amongst the living understand this. Most believe themselves to be already wide awake and think they actually are kings and servants!

A modern analogy that helps me get the message of the mystics is to compare life to watching a movie. Most of the time I completely identify with "Tim," who is the hero of my particular movie. The downside of this is that I actually believe that the bad things that he endures during his adventures are actually happening to me. The saints and sages, however, have shown me that I am, in reality, sitting securely in the auditorium. My essential Self is a passive witness of Tim's joys and woes. I exist outside of the whole drama. When the narrative ends and the movie is wound up

and returned to its box it may be sad, because I find the story wonderfully compelling, but it will not be tragic. No one in the movie can really die, because no one was really alive in the first place.

This analogy does not mean I dismiss life as a worthless illusion. That would be like sitting in an auditorium completely aware that the movie I am watching is no more than colored light flickering on a screen. If I did this, I would no longer be seduced into the adventure at all, which would make watching the film an unenjoyable waste of time.

I don't feel that the mystics want me to withdraw from life, but simply to realize that I am in the world but not of it. They want me to do what I naturally do when I actually go to see a movie. I treat the experience as an illusion to be entered into and enjoyed, while remaining tacitly aware that I am not actually the hero of the movie, but utterly safe in the auditorium. This makes the good parts of the adventure great and the scary parts exciting, rather than terrifying.

When I approach living my life in the same way, I allow myself to fully enter into the illusion of being the body in the world, while tacitly remaining aware that my essential being is forever untouched by the dramas of life.

In my experience, to glimpse that I am "in the world but not of it" is comparatively easy, but to sustain the vision is immensely difficult. The habit of identifying with the physical body is hard to break. But the saints and sages suggest that if we approach life as a journey of awakening, it will become a process of transformation that gradually turns us into the type of person capable of sustaining the transcendental vision of our true impersonal nature. We need to enter into the dream of life because it is through the unfolding drama of being in the world that we can come to understand that we are not of it. It provides the necessary opportunities to awaken to our deeper identity and progressively learn to sustain this awareness.

Ironically, I have found that, far from leading to withdrawal, being aware that my essential nature is not "of the world" allows me to engage unreservedly with the dramas of my life. When I identify with my body I become easily frightened and try to avoid the challenges my life offers me. But the more I know myself to be not "of the world" and essentially safe, the more I am able to embrace the life process, with all its suffering and sorrows.

DEATH AND RESURRECTION

The saints and sages teach that to realize our true immortal nature we must die while we are still alive. Plato describes the "true philosopher" as someone who "makes dying his way of life." The Zen masters urge, "While living be a dead man." St. Paul writes, "I die daily." The Hindu saint Kabir writes, "It is those who are dead while living who shall never die." The Christian mystic St. John of the Cross announces: "I live without inhabiting myself in such a way that I am dying so that I do not die." The Gnostic Christian sage Valentinus teaches: "From the beginning we are immortal children of Eternal Life. We choose to die so that we can annihilate death completely."

The mystics want us to "die" to the idea of ourselves as a body, so that we will "resurrect" as our true Self. The ancient Pagans portrayed these teachings mythologically in their many stories of a dying and resurrecting Godman, which we have inherited as the story of Jesus. The Greek word that is translated "resurrect" in these myths also means "awaken." To "die" now is to see through the illusion of being the body. To "resurrect" is to wake up and realize we are Consciousness.

If we die and resurrect, the saints and sages teach, we will discover something utterly astonishing. There is one Dreamer of the dream of life. Although in the dream we appear to be separate individuals, actually there is one Self, which is the Self of All. One Big Mind within which everything exists as an appearance. One Infinite Love that holds all that is in its warm embrace. When we spiritually awaken and see through the illusion of separateness, we understand that there is only God. The Sufi master Abd al-Kader explains:

There are two types of death. One which is inevitable and common to all, and one which is voluntary and experienced by the few. It is the second death which Muhammad prescribed saying "Die before you die." Those who die this voluntary death are resurrected. All the business of their lives returns to the Oneness of God. As the Prophet said, "You will not see your Lord until you are dead." This is because it is through this death and resurrection that everything becomes nothing and only One thing exists. One Reality.

The teaching that essentially everything exists as the expression of One Big Mind is the foundation of the perennial philosophy. We will put off exploring this further until Chapter 6, *Big Mind*, because it is a very big idea that can be difficult to fully comprehend. Like so many of the insights of the saints and sages, however, this is only because it is actually so extremely simple. For now, we need only be aware that for the mystics our apparent separateness is an illusion. All beings are the expressions of One Being.

DEATH IS SAFE

When we change how we think, we change how we feel. If we think of ourselves merely as a mortal body, then it is no surprise that we fear death. If, however, we understand life as a journey of awakening to our immortal Self, then death becomes a challenge, not a tragedy—the supreme opportunity to see through the illusion of separateness and recognize our true nature to be the glorious Love and immaculate Intelligence that permeates all and is the source of all.

Rumi teaches: "Your fear of death is actually fear of confronting your Self." Death brings us face to face with the Mystery of Existence—our true eternal nature. We fear this because it is unfamiliar. The secret to overcoming fear and preparing for death is to cultivate an awareness of our essential Self while alive. If we do so, the saints and sages assure us, we will find that the Mystery we feared is all love.

Death is not a meaningless end. It is the great initiation toward which life is leading. It is the opportunity to cast off the body, like an old overcoat when the warm weather comes, and enter naked into the radiant emptiness of pure Consciousness. The Buddhist sage Longchenpa explains:

My delight in death exceeds the pleasure of a merchant who makes a vast fortune, or a victorious war god, or a sage in deep meditation. Like a traveler taking to the road, I will leave this world and return home to the limitless bliss of deathlessness. My life is completed and my karma is done with. There is no more to be gained by praying. Things of the world are abandoned. The show is over. In the pure afterdeath states I will instantly realize the essence of my Being. I am approaching the ground of primal perfection.

When we stop approaching dying as a grim catastrophe, we can lighten up a little. I always tried my best to be sensitive to the suffering of those I visited as a death and bereavement counselor. Yet I often found that my unwillingness to go along with the idea that death was an awful tragedy allowed not only moments of real and poignant sorrow, but also the unexpected relief of lightness and laughter.

While for most of us, death is not a laughing matter, something that marks out the spiritually mature is that their fundamental confidence in the benign nature of existence enables them to smile at the absurdity of their predicament, no matter how bleak. It is not denial or self-deception to let go of the seriousness of the situation. It is recognizing a deeper reality behind the appearances. It is knowing that life is good, even when it is also bad. It is understanding that death is safe.

Those who see death for what it is can let it be just what it is, without turning it into a depressing drama. When the Greek philosopher Socrates was condemned to die by the Athenian authorities for unsettling citizens with his relentless questioning, he remained cheerful to the end. As he drank a cup of poison, his friend Crito asked "Where shall we bury you?" Socrates answered "Anywhere you like, if you can catch me!"

The Taoist Sage T'ao Ch'ien advises:

Just surrender to the wave of the Great Change. Neither pulling anything to you nor pushing anything away. And when it is time to go, then simply go. Don't make a big deal out of it.

In the Zen tradition it used to be expected that masters would write a final verse of insightful poetry just before they died. One Zen master was almost passing away and had not performed this requirement, which his students urged him to undertake. Eventually, before letting out his last breath, he reluctantly took a pen and scrawled:

Life is thus.
Death is thus.
Verse or no verse,
what's the fuss?

MEDITATION 3

The Unborn Emptiness of Consciousness

Rumi writes "At death only knowledge of emptiness will be your rations to sustain you on the road." The only way to truly mitigate our fear of death is to become aware now, while we are alive, of being the unborn emptiness of Consciousness. This meditation exercise is designed to help you do just that.

Preparation
- Sit quietly in a position you find comfortable. Be relaxed but alert.
- Close your eyes and rest your attention on your breath as it comes and goes. Let your breath settle into a slow and regular pattern as you let go of all agitation.

Meditation

PART 1
- Become aware of yourself as the witness of thoughts. Imagine yourself as the empty space of Consciousness within which thoughts come and go, like clouds passing across a clear blue sky.
- Watch your thoughts as they emerge from the darkness of your depths and dissipate again. Don't let your awareness fixate on a thought, but simply witness your thoughts as objects within Consciousness.

PART 2
- Open your eyes and become aware of yourself as the witness of sensations. What can you see, hear, smell, taste, and feel? Imagine yourself as the empty space of Consciousness within which these sensations have their existence.
- Become aware of your body as part of your sensual experience. Imagine yourself as the empty space of Consciousness within which the body has its existence as sensation. Don't contract your awareness into the body, but let the body be in you.

PART 3

- Become aware of yourself as the witness of both thoughts and sensations. Imagine yourself as the empty space of Consciousness that embraces all that you experience.

- Be aware of your experience as a unified whole. Watch thoughts and sensations moving and transforming as one metamorphosing totality.

- You are the witness of the Oneness. You are Consciousness that contains the cosmos. You are eternity that contains the flow of time. You are permanence aware of change. You are the Mystery within which all arises.

MEDITATION 4

Being In the World but Not of It

As a body you are "in the world," but as Consciousness you are "not of it." This meditation exercise builds on the previous exercise to help you explore these teachings experientially.

Preparation

- Sit quietly in a position you find comfortable. Be relaxed but alert.
- Keep your eyes open. Focus your vision gently on a spot somewhere in front of you, but let your awareness be diffuse and ambient rather than concentrated.

Meditation

PART 1

- Become aware of your apparent identity as a physical body in the world. Describe your apparent bodily identity to yourself. Be aware that it takes time to list all its many qualities and characteristics.
- Now become aware of your essential nature as Consciousness. Be aware that it is an emptiness that can only be apperceived immediately in the present moment.
- Become aware that as a body you are a complex of changing qualities existing in time, but as Consciousness you are simply Being in eternity.
- Practice moving between an awareness of your essential identity as Consciousness and your apparent identity as the body. Breathe out and be aware of yourself as the emptiness of Consciousness that contains the cosmos. Breathe in and become aware of yourself as a particular person within the cosmos. Breathe in and out. Be ineffable Consciousness witnessing itself appearing to be a physical body.

PART 2

- Imagine the flow of your experience as an adventure movie you are watching, in which your personal identity is the hero.

- Experiment with completely identifying with the hero of the action. Contemplate how this inevitably leads to pain and suffering, because you will believe that the bad things the hero endures are actually happening to you.

- Now experiment with identifying solely with witnessing Consciousness and disregard your experience as an illusion, as if you were sitting in an auditorium completely aware that the movie you are watching is no more than flickering pictures on a screen. Contemplate how this makes watching the movie completely meaningless and unenjoyable.

- Consider how, when you actually watch a movie you treat it as an illusion to be entered into and enjoyed, while you remain tacitly aware that you are not actually the hero of the movie, but utterly safe in the auditorium, and that this makes the good parts of the adventure great and the scary parts exciting.

- Imagine approaching your life in the same way. Be in the movie but not of it. Allow yourself to fully enter into the illusion of being the body in the world, while tacitly remaining aware that your essential being is forever untouched by the dramas of life.

- Notice that the more you are confident of your essential safety as the unborn witness, the more you feel able to abandon yourself to the joy, suffering, learning, failing, growing, and death that the adventure of life entails.

The Afterlife and Reincarnation

Why should we not assume that life and death are equally good? Death is to life what returning is to going away. Death is a return to where we set out from when we were born. Clinging to life and fearing death is crazy, because they are two successive phases of the same process.

Lin Lei
Taoist sage

The perennial philosophy teaches that we are unborn and undying Consciousness, which witnessed our birth and which will witness our death. But what will we witness after death? What will we experience when the body dies? To answer this, let's begin by examining the extraordinary testimonies of those who claim to have died and yet returned to tell the tale. Such stories were recorded centuries ago by Plato and the Venerable Bede. In recent decades, however, they have become very common as more people have been resuscitated by modern medicine, even after they have been declared clinically dead. These apparent sorties of the living into the afterlife have become known as "Near-Death Experiences" or NDEs. Researchers have found that NDEs often follow a very similar pattern. Let's examine the typical NDE and see if it sheds any light on what awaits us after death.

Most NDEs begin with people experiencing a heart attack or an accident, and suddenly finding themselves outside their body. Often they describe looking on as friends or doctors rush around trying to revive them. They can hear and see all that is happening, but they feel peaceful and detached, no longer consumed by the drama of dying. They experience their body as an object with which they no longer identify and watch impassively as it is pronounced dead. L remembers this moment in her NDE.

At this point I just popped out of my body and I suddenly feel great. I was in so much pain, but all the pain was gone. And for once I'm just me. Me myself. No one's wife, mother, or daughter. I'm completely myself for the first time.

Next the world of the living starts to fade and the "dead" person becomes aware of a tunnel with a bright light at the end, which emanates overwhelming love and wellbeing.

   People often describe the Light as God or Christ or Buddha or Krishna, depending on their cultural expectations. R is a tough-looking guy, covered with tattoos, who had been shot in the chest while a young soldier in Vietnam, but I remember him recalling his experience of the Light with tears of wonder in his eyes.

I was laying on the stretcher and I was suddenly out of my body. And I was above myself. At that time I turned and what I knew to be a brick wall turned into the most beautiful, loving Light that I have ever seen or witnessed or felt in my whole life. And this Love-Light just surrounded me. And I stayed with the Light for a while just lapping up the love. I felt so peaceful and calm. All the pain was gone. Everything was right.

As the "deceased" is drawn toward the Love-Light they are welcomed by their friends and family who have died before them. Those they meet are happy and appear as they were in the prime of their lives. They no longer suffer from any physical afflictions, but appear in what is sometimes described as a "body of light" or "spirit body." This is often a joyous reunion in a heavenly paradise, described as a beautiful meadow with a stream.

The next phase of the NDE is known as the "life-review." The person relives, in a timeless immediate way, the life they have just lived. But now they are a detached observer, able to learn from their mistakes, see the opportunities they missed, and the effects of their actions upon others. L relates:

I had the whole of my life go before me from the very moment of life to this very point. This whole panorama. I was part of it. I was moving in it. But I was also seeing it. And the things that you think of as being so important are not important at all. It's the little things that really count. Whether you are kind to one another. I was just surrounded by love. Pulsating.

At some point in the NDE the person is told by the Love-Light or their friends or relatives that they have to go back, because they have further "work to do." Some people desperately want to return and ask to do so, usually because they have responsibilities to loved ones who depend on them. Researchers have also found that approximately half of all children who experience an NDE want to go back to be with their mommy and daddy. But the majority of people want to stay in the love and peace of the afterlife and have no desire to go back to the limited physical body they have left behind.

When they return to the body, people recall their NDE as a blessing, and often feel it has transformed them into more caring and compassionate people, with a powerful sense of purpose in their life—as does R, who enthuses about the Light.

When you experience the Love-Light, the total unconditional love,
the unmotivated love of God, then you have really experienced
what life is all about.

Most people find it impossible to doubt that their NDE has given them a glimpse
of what awaits us when we die and claim to have completely lost the fear of
death—even to welcome it. B explains "The act of dying can be painful and gross,
but death itself is only beautiful." L urges "Look forward to death. It is the most
wonderful experience."

FACT OR FANTASY?

When I first came across reports of NDEs, many years ago, I remember being extremely moved by these stories and inspired by the passionate optimism of those who told them. They touched me in such a deep place that I had an intuitive conviction that they were, indeed, authentic glimpses of the afterlife. The NDE phenomenon is now well known, and has been studied by many people who have been similarly moved and inspired. But, as NDEs have been studied in greater depth, some scientists have questioned whether they really tell us anything about life after death at all.

The most obvious reason for this is that they are *near-death* experiences, not death experiences. Although these people may have been declared dead, they were subsequently revived. They didn't actually die. These experiences, it is argued, may well tell us something about the dying process, but cannot tell us anything about death. And what they tell us about dying is that, unable to face the reality of death, we retreat into a sort of wish-fulfilling fantasy. Or possibly NDEs are hallucinations caused by the drugs administered to the patient for pain relief? Or the result of what happens in the brain under extreme conditions, such as the oxygen starvation experienced when the heart stops working? As for the tunnel and the Light—experiences like this can be deliberately induced by putting people into certain vigorous flight-simulators.

These criticisms, however, don't necessarily undermine the validity of the NDE. The fact that patients are revived doesn't mean they didn't temporarily enter alternative planes of reality to this one. Mystics and shamans, who specialize in the exploration of Consciousness, report making journeys into such realms while they are still living in this world. Many of the recipients of an NDE have had no drugs administered to them, so their experiences can't simply be dismissed as chemically induced hallucinations. The fact that experiences somewhat similar to the NDE can be induced proves nothing.

Spiritual practices, such as meditation, Tai Chi Chuan, yoga, and so on (not to mention the Shamanic use of psychedelic power plants!), all change the bodily state of the practitioner to induce altered states of Consciousness. The fact that these states are induced or correlate to changes in brain chemistry does not mean they are somehow unreal. From the findings of science it would appear that all states of awareness correlate to activity in the brain, but this does not mean they are identical to this brain activity any more than the electrical activity in your television is identical with the program you are watching, which exists on the airwaves quite independently of the television that receives the signal.

Materialist explanations do not account for "objective" evidence that appears to validate the NDE. For example, some people describe leaving their "dead" body in the operating room and, in the out-of-body state, slipping into another room where they try to comfort their distraught relatives. After they are revived they are able to accurately relate not only what the doctors said and did while they were clinically dead, but even what friends and relatives said and did in other rooms. Other "objective" evidence includes people who have returned from their NDE with information they did not previously possess. For example, L relates meeting in the "afterlife" a baby brother she never knew she had. On her return she questioned her father and found out there had indeed been a little boy who died before she was born.

For some scientists, however, the problem with all such evidence is that it is anecdotal. It can be collated but not tested and is, therefore, potentially unreliable. People easily fantasize. We all know how memories change over time and we easily end up believing what we want to believe. Yet the anecdotal evidence is compelling. Accounts of NDEs are remarkably consistent and widespread. Researchers have estimated that as many as eight million people have had an NDE in the United States alone. And NDEs don't just happen to certain types of people who may be already predisposed to supernatural experiences. They happen to religious people and atheists, agnostics and scientists, the educated and the uneducated, the rich and the poor, adults and children. They happen to the very pillars of society whose anecdotal evidence would be taken very seriously in a court of law.

I find it hard to dismiss, for example, the testimony of Carl Jung, one of the founding fathers of modern psychotherapy and a personal friend of some of the great scientists of his day. After a heart attack he felt that he had, without doubt, experienced something of what lies beyond the grave. He writes:

What happens after death is so unspeakably glorious that our imagination and feelings do not suffice to form even an approximate conception of it.

The other reason I feel we should not dismiss NDEs as irrelevant fantasies is that they resonate with the teachings of the saints and sages, who also suggest that at death we will encounter a Love-Light, undergo a life-review, and enter other realms of experience, which Christians call heavens and hells, Hindus call lokas and talas, and Tibetan Buddhists call bardos. Let's now examine the spiritual perspective on what will happen to us after death.

DEATH AND REBIRTH

The perennial philosophy teaches that at death our habitual identification with the body is shattered and we have the supreme opportunity to become enlightened, by recognizing our true ineffable identity as the emptiness of pure Consciousness. According to *The Tibetan Book of the Dead*, after death we will experience our true Self or Buddha-nature as a "Clear Light." This remarkable Buddhist scripture counsels the dying person:

Your breathing is about to cease. Your guru has previously tried to reveal to you the Clear Light of Consciousness. Now you are about to come face to face with the Clear Light in reality. Consciousness is like an empty, cloudless sky. A naked, transparent void, without circumference or center. Know this to be your Self and abide in that state.

Listen. You are now experiencing the radiance of the Clear Light of Pure Reality. Recognize it as your own Consciousness, without form, characteristics, or color. Naturally void. The supreme Reality. The All-Good. Your own awareness is emptiness. Not nothingness, but pure Consciousness itself, unobstructed, shining, and blissful. Consciousness is the Beneficent Buddha.

Your own Consciousness, without form and empty, is inseparable from the shining, blissful Light. Being one with it is perfect enlightenment. Your own Consciousness, shining, void, and inseparable from the great body of Radiance, has no birth, nor death. It is the immutable Light—Buddha Amitabha.

This is all you need to know. Recognizing the voidness of your own Consciousness is Buddhahood. If you recognize your own Consciousness, you will be in the divine Consciousness of the Buddha.

According to *The Tibetan Book of the Dead*, if we are spiritually mature enough to recognize the Love-Light as our own deeper nature we will consciously merge with it. If not, at a certain point we will find it impossible to stay conscious any longer and unconsciously merge with the Light, after which we will find ourselves "reborn." The continuation of experience after death in a different form is known as reincarnation or reembodiment. The body we once believed ourselves to be has died, but if we fail to recognize ourselves to be the Clear Light of Consciousness, we now identify with the new form we appear to be.

The purpose of dying and reincarnating is that it changes the conditions within which we make our journey of awakening, and so gives us a new opportunity, in a new environment, as a new "person," to realize our true ineffable nature. If we didn't die it would be much harder, perhaps impossible, to awaken. We would have no reason to question our identification with the body and would become more and more embroiled in the illusion that we are the particular person we appear to be. Shunryu Suzuki teaches: "We should be very grateful to have a limited body, like mine and yours. If you had limitless life it would be a real problem for you."

The doctrine of reincarnation is usually associated with Hinduism and Buddhism, but it is taught by mystics from all spiritual traditions, including the Islamic Sufis, the Jewish Kabbalists, and the Christian Gnostics. The mistake that is often made in understanding reincarnation is presuming it means that we come back *here*. But from the mystical perspective *here* is a sort of dream. We may indeed reincarnate back into this communal dream we call the world, but this is not the only option.

The perennial philosophy suggests there is an infinite number of possible dream worlds that we can experience on our journey of awakening. Death and rebirth is the process of moving between them. The end of one adventure within Consciousness is the beginning of the next. Just as life is a cycle of many days and nights, so existence is the greater cycle of many deaths and rebirths, through which we progressively awaken. Socrates uses this analogy to convince his audience that there is life after death. Here is an abridged form of his argument.

Let's approach the question of survival after death like this. The ancient teachings tell us that at death the soul goes to another world and then returns here again. If this is true and the living come from the dead, then our souls must survive death, for otherwise how could they be born again? So, if we could clearly ascertain that the living were once dead, then we would have conclusive proof that the soul survives death. Do you agree with that?

Think about this. Isn't everything that has an opposite created from that opposite? There is any number of examples. Anything which becomes bigger must first of all be smaller. And something which gets smaller must first of all have been bigger. Things become weaker after they have been stronger. And things get faster only by first being slower. And something worse was once better. Do you see what I am saying? And do you see that this is universally true for all opposites?

So think about it. Sleep is the opposite of waking. So sleeping comes from waking and waking comes from sleeping. They generate each other. Do you agree with me so far? Now let's analyze death in the same way. Death is the opposite of life. So death and life must generate each other. What comes after life? Death does. And what comes after death? Life does. We are forced to conclude that the living come from the dead. This means that after death our souls exist in some other world. If the dead come from the living and the living from the dead then the souls of the dead must exist somewhere from which they can return.

KARMA

The perennial philosophy teaches that the character of our next life depends on the life we have just lived. Our future experience is a product of how much we have embraced the opportunities our present life offers us to spiritually awaken. The *Srimad Bhagavatam*, a Hindu scripture, teaches:

At the moment of death all of a man's experiences of life on earth come into Consciousness, for in Consciousness are stored all impressions of past deeds. Then comes complete loss of memory and there arises in Consciousness a vision of his life to come. This complete forgetfulness of past identity is death and the complete acceptance of another state and identification with a new body is rebirth. Though he existed before, he considers himself newly born. But his new life is a product of his deeds in his previous life.

The life-review in the NDE suggests that a type of self-judgment occurs after death, which determines the nature of our next birth. But various spiritual traditions teach that this self-judgment is often unconscious and experienced as the hand of fate. The Chinese sage Confucius explains:

A being dies over and over again. It receives a particular form for the duration of a particular existence, which is equivalent to the active period of daytime. Then it dies, which is equivalent to resting at night. And so it continues through the chain of time. What sort of new being it becomes depends on its spiritual merit, but it rarely comprehends this process which it experiences as the hand of fate.

According to the perennial philosophy our present experience is always the result of our previous experience and how we reacted to it. In Indian philosophy this is

called karma. St. Paul teaches the same doctrine when he writes, "As you sow so shall you reap." The past is the seed of our present experience and our future will be the fruit of the present. Scientific materialists recognize the principle of causal determinism but limit its operation to the physical world, which is all they believe exists. The perennial philosophy has an expanded notion of causality. It teaches that everything, including thoughts, intentions, emotions, and so on, causally effect our future experience. This process continues after the death of the body, so that our post-death experience is conditioned by the life we lead now.

Karma is a much misunderstood concept. It is often imagined as a system of cosmic justice that explains our present predicament as a reward or punishment for our good and bad actions in the past, both in this life and in previous incarnations. It is more insightful, however, to understand karma as the natural process whereby life presents us with the challenges and opportunities we need to awaken. Our karma is our curriculum in the school of life, which mirrors back to us our spiritual immaturity so that we can gradually spiritually mature.

In Christian terms, karma is the "wages of sin" that prevents us from experiencing "Eternal Life." The word "sin" is a translation of a Greek term from archery, which means "to miss the mark." Sin is the result of our assumption that we are the body, which inevitably results in selfish thoughts and actions that "miss the mark" of complete goodness. Sin is another word for our ignorance, which keeps us bound to the cycle of death and rebirth. We experience "Eternal Life" when we awaken to our timeless, unborn, essential nature as Consciousness.

The basic idea of karma is very simple—the future emerges from the past through a great web of causality—but the way that karma works out in any particular life is infinitely complex. Each of us must make sense of the idiosyncrasies of our own fate for ourselves, because it is a product of our unique karmic curriculum, which meets the specific needs of the unique journey of awakening that defines our individuality.

The Buddhist master Drakpa Gyaltsen laments, "Most human beings prepare for the future all their lives, yet meet the next life totally unprepared." The saints and sages suggest that, if we understand the process of karma and reincarnation, we will take a longer-term view and approach our present life as an opportunity to sow the seeds of our next life, through spiritually awakening. The *Adi Granth*, a Sikh scripture, teaches: "O shrewd businessman, do only profitable business: deal only in that commodity which shall accompany you after death."

REMEMBERING AND FORGETTING

If we have lived before, one thing is for certain: most of us have forgotten about it. If in a future life we forget all about this life, can we really regard reincarnation as survival of death? I don't see why not. We think of ourselves as the same individual as the baby that we have developed from into adulthood, although we have no recollection of our very early years. We accept this memory loss because

we feel that these early experiences, although now forgotten, form the foundation of our later personality. Can we understand the relationship between past lives and our present life in the same way? Although we don't consciously remember our past lives, they condition and form the foundation of what we have become today.

We fear death as the great forgetting. But perhaps we should see life as forgetting and death as remembering. Accounts of NDEs suggest that at death we will remember all the details of our life that we have long since forgotten. The saints and sages suggest that if we are aware enough we will remember not only our present life but our past lives also. Death is remembering. Reincarnation is forgetting what we have previously experienced, in

order to undergo new experiences, in a new environment, as a new person, which affords us new opportunities to awaken.

If death is remembering and birth is forgetting, perhaps it is being born, rather than dying, that we should fear. Or perhaps there is nothing to fear at all. After all, we don't normally worry about temporary periods of forgetfulness, as for instance when we get very drunk! And we don't fear forgetting this world and everyone within it each night when we go to sleep. Forgetting doesn't seem to be bad if we feel assured of remembering again later. The perennial philosophy teaches that, like everything else, memories exist in Consciousness and so are not lost forever with the demise of the brain. From the spiritual perspective, the cycle of death and reincarnation is a cycle of remembering and forgetting, through which we come to finally remember what we truly are.

The Pagan philosopher Pythagoras called the cycle of death and rebirth the "Wheel of Suffering" and the Buddha called it the "Wheel of Grief." This is because it is identification with the body that lives and dies that is the source of all grief and suffering. We are trapped on the wheel as long as we continue to forget our true nature and identify with the different bodily forms we appear to be in each incarnation, rather than with the Clear Light of the Consciousness, which witnesses life, death, and rebirth. For as the scholar and mystic Dr. W. Y. Evans-Wentz explains, "The Knower itself neither incarnates nor reincarnates—it is the Spectator."

The message of the mystics is this. This world is a communal dream in Consciousness. Death is the end of one dream and rebirth is the beginning of another. The purpose of dreaming is for you to awaken to your true identity as the Dreamer. Then you will realize that "Everything you experience is a product of your imagination, for in reality nothing exists outside of you," as The Tibetan Book of the Dead puts it.

Those who wake up from the dream and realize they are the Dreamer transcend the cycle of death and rebirth, because they know they are essentially unborn and undying. They understand that they are not the body that is born and dies, but unchanging eternal Consciousness. Zen master Ikkyu once visited a dying student to ask if he required any help understanding these teachings. The student replied, "I don't need anything. I am just going to the Changeless." Ikkyu replied, "If you think you are a something that can go somewhere, you still need my teachings."

MEDITATION 5

A Near-Death Experience

This meditation is a way of imaginatively exploring the NDE and the new perspective on our present life that it offers.

Preparation
- Lie down quietly in a position you find comfortable. Be relaxed but alert.
- Close your eyes and rest your attention on your breath as it comes and goes. Let your breath settle into a slow and regular pattern as you let go of all agitation.

Meditation
- Imagine that you have unexpectedly experienced a heart attack and your heart has stopped beating. What are you thinking and feeling?
- Now imagine that all the pain ceases and you find yourself out of your body, looking down on the physical form you have previously taken to be you.
- How do you feel about your body?
- You now see a tunnel before you, at the end of which is a bright light emanating loving kindness and utter tranquillity. What are your reactions to the Love-Light?
- Let yourself be drawn down the tunnel toward the Light and bathe in the love and peace for a while.
- Out of the Light emerge some figures who may be friends and family who have already died. Who are they and what do they say to you?
- You now find yourself reviewing your past life. Take some time to remember your life journey from birth to this present moment.
- Which events stand out for you as important and why?
- What do you regret and what are you pleased to remember?
- What do you feel you have learned from your life?
- What do you feel you have failed to learn from your life?

- You now hear a voice emanating from the Love-Light saying that you must return to your body, because there is more work for you to do. How do you feel about going back?
- What is the work you feel you still have to do?
- Find yourself back in your body, which now feels healthy and full of wellbeing.
- What have you learned from this experience?
- Has it changed what you want to do with the rest of your life?
- When you are ready open your eyes and write down your thoughts and feelings, so that you can contemplate them, now and at some later date.

MEDITATION 6

Waves on the Ocean

In the British Isles, where I live, many people go to live by the sea in their old age. This feels entirely appropriate to me. There's something about the vast emptiness of the sea, and the rhythm of its waves and tides, which speaks of death, eternity, and the Cycles of Existence. For this meditation I suggest you make a visit to the ocean, if that is possible. If not, close your eyes and imagine yourself on the shore gazing out across the ocean.

Preparation

- If you are by the ocean, walk in a state of quiet contemplation along the shoreline. If you are meditating, sit in a position you find comfortable, with your eyes closed, and imagine you are by the sea.

- Rest your attention on your breath as it comes and goes. Let your breath settle into a slow and regular pattern as you let go of all agitation.

Meditation

- As you watch the waves wash up onto the shore and retreat into the ocean once again, contemplate all the cycles of nature. The cycle of the year as the seasons complete their eternal course. The food chain in which all life feeds off the death of other life and then, in turn, itself becomes food. The cycle of sleep and waking. And the cycle of life, death, and rebirth.

- Imagine yourself to be a wave on the ocean. Each morning your awareness comes crashing onto the shoreline of your waking world and each night it retreats back to the silent depths.

- Imagine your whole life to be a wave, running up upon the shoreline in youth, turning at middle age, then pulling you back into the ocean from which you came in old age and death, only to come surging back once again, and again, and again. Watch as each wave arises from the one before, both different and yet a continuation of the same eternal wave.

- Imagine your permanent identity as the still and unmoving hidden depths from which the waves emerge.

- Imagine yourself to be the whole ocean. Your individuality is a wave on the Ocean of Oneness. We are different movements on the surface of the deep, which is our shared essential nature. The Hindu sage Janaka teaches:

How remarkable! In Me the limitless ocean, the waves of individual selves arise according to their inherent nature, meet and play with one another for a while, and then disappear.

OLD AGE AND ILLNESS

Your pain is the breaking of the shell that encloses your
understanding.
Even as the stone of the fruit must break, that its heart may stand in
the sun, so must you know pain.
And could you keep your heart in wonder at the daily miracles of
your life, your pain would not seem less wondrous than your joy;
And you would accept the seasons of your heart, even as you have
always accepted the seasons that pass over your fields.
And you would watch with serenity through the winters of your
grief.

Kahlil Gibran
Poet and mystic

Death may be "safe," as the perennial philosophy teaches, but the fact
of suffering remains. For some people it is not death that is frightening, but the
suffering that may precede it. Old age and illness present us with the unwelcome
prospect of the gradual decline of our physical functions. For those who believe
themselves to be the body, this is a cruel and meaningless end. For those with
a spiritual perspective, however, it is the final opportunity to awaken before death
puts us "face to face" with the Love-Light, which is our true essential
nature. The Taoist sage Lieh Tzu teaches "Hardship, old age, and death
are regarded as the bane of human life, but the
wise accept them as necessary parts of the
process of existence."

In our materialist culture old age has no value. It is the failure to stay young and active. The old are "out-of-date" and redundant. Their life is seen as no longer having a purpose. They are an inconvenience to be hidden out of sight in old people's homes, where they can live out their remaining days playing banal games and watching television. But this is not so in all cultures.

In India, for example, life is traditionally divided into four phases, which lead through childhood, to adulthood, to full maturity, to being an elder. In the final stage the person becomes a sannyasi or renunciate, who gives up his or her preoccupation with the world and concentrates on the spiritual life as a preparation for death. Aboriginal elders, likewise, will often leave their community in old age and retreat alone into the mountains, where they prepare for death by practicing various techniques such as "sky gazing," which involves staring into the empty sky to become aware of the spaciousness of Consciousness.

Without this spiritual understanding of the purpose of old age, the last phase of life becomes a meaningless pantomime full of bitterness and regret. Carl Jung declares:

> As a physician I am convinced that it is hygienic to discover in death a goal toward which one can strive; and that shrinking from it is something unhealthy and abnormal which robs the second half of life of its purpose.

In old age, the only challenge left to face is the greatest of all challenges. A challenge our life has been progressively preparing us to face. Toward the end of his life the Renaissance genius and Platonic mystic Leonardo da Vinci observed, "All the time I thought I was learning how to live, I was learning how to die."

Like every phase of life, old age has its particular gifts to offer us, if we are aware enough to recognize them. The pain and deterioration that accompany old age and illness are undoubtedly hard to endure, but the saints and sages encourage us to welcome the opportunities to awaken that they present us with, as part of our karmic curriculum of awakening.

In many spiritual traditions seekers deliberately court suffering through ascetic practices, so that they can learn endurance and transcendence. This may seem perverse (and in extreme cases it is!), but asceticism arises from the understanding that suffering is a powerful spiritual initiation. If we analyze the debilitating process of old age and illness dispassionately for a moment, they can be seen as a naturally occurring form of ascetic practice.

As part of my own spiritual search I have experimented with long periods of meditation, in which I sat quietly while withdrawing my attention from my senses and clearing my mind of thoughts and memories. What happens in old age? Our senses begin to fail us, so that we can no longer see and hear very well. We find it hard to get around and become immobile. Our memory and intellect become enfeebled and we find it more difficult to think. Old age puts us into an ideal condition for meditative practice.

The saints and sages encourage us to continually contemplate our own death, as a spiritual practice to help us awaken. I have often spent periods attempting to come to terms with my mortality, but I remember it dawning on me one day that, while for me this was an optional spiritual practice, for my father, who has experienced an acute heart attack and is in his late seventies, the awareness of death is now a daily reality. He is living with the possibility of death in a way that I can only imagine. While any of us can die at any minute, he knows that his imminent death is becoming increasingly likely. His life has led him, through the natural process of aging, to practice the awareness of death. He sometimes finds this depressing. But often it has the opposite effect, making him more appreciative of life, more loving and open, less willing to become stressed by unimportant trivia, and more intent on enjoying the moment.

When physical deterioration is thought of as an unmitigated evil, we may hope that we don't have to endure a slow and drawn out death. Yet are those who die quickly luckier than those who do not? Not necessarily, if the dying process is seen as a preparation for our encounter with the Love-Light of Consciousness.

As the body disintegrates we are given the opportunity to gradually relinquish the many identities we have built upon the foundation of believing ourselves to be the physical body. We may define ourselves by our job or social role, but as the body deteriorates we are forced to retire from work and our social commitments. We may define ourselves as a sexual being, but as the body declines sexuality fades. We may define ourselves as someone who is in control, but eventually we may become totally reliant on others for our physical needs. This painful deconstruction is the tearing down of the prison walls, which leads to liberation. It invites us to discover the essential Self that remains after all of our temporary pseudoidentities have been stripped away, and so prepares us for death and the encounter with the Clear Light of Consciousness.

Human beings are compelled to find meaning in their lives. When life seems meaningless it is hard to endure. Most of us find meaning by giving ourselves goals to fulfill. But the old and the ill know in advance that their aspirations have no possibility of being fulfilled. Men sometimes die soon after retiring from work because they are faced with the apparent meaninglessness of no longer having anything to achieve. Spirituality, however, gives this phase of our lives meaning. Old age and illness require us to willingly abandon our personal agendas and surrender to life's great agenda, which is to awaken us to who we really are.

Of course, if we have not prepared for the spiritual opportunities that old age and illness present us with while in good health, this enforced retreat from the world is difficult to take advantage of. This is why the saints and sages encourage us to cultivate attitudes and practices that nurture our awakening while we are young. Yet, I have met old people who have never undertaken any spiritual practices who have nevertheless naturally become serene and accepting as they have approached death, quieting down into a sublime state of tranquillity, emanating silent wisdom and actionless compassion. Aging has not made them less alive, but more alive in a new way. As the Buddhist teacher Stephen Levine observes, "The old who live in their bodies are bent under the strain. The old who live in their hearts are aglow."

SUFFERING IS GRACE

From the spiritual perspective, suffering is an aspect of our karmic curriculum of awakening to be embraced, not feared. Suffering is gritty grace. It is a gift from God that shows us our vulnerability and compels us to search for answers. It is just as much a blessing as our apparent good fortune, because all our experiences are designed to help us awaken. Suffering is a harsh but powerful teacher on the spiritual path, who reveals where we are holding tightly to the illusion of identifying with the body. Suffering may seem like the problem, but in forcing us to fully face our predicament, it is also a part of the solution. Rumi explains:

Suffering is a gift for in it is hidden mercy. Allah gave Pharaoh so much wealth that he imagined himself to be divine. In his whole life he never experienced spiritual heartache, so he never felt the need to call to Allah. Allah gave him the greatest empire in the world, but he gave him no grief, pain, or sorrow. But grief is better than an empire because it compels us to secretly call to Allah.

Rumi tells the story of a soul at death who reached the gates of Heaven, where Allah observed with consternation, "You are the same as when you left! You were blessed by a life full of opportunities, so where are the bruises and scars left by your journey?" Life is a learning experience and it is impossible to learn without getting a bit battered and bruised, both physically and emotionally.

Rumi is not suggesting that suffering is desirable. By definition suffering is the undesirable. He is saying that it brings the desirable with it. Suffering may not be something we would chose, but when it comes it brings with it the opportunity to awaken. When we can see that "suffering has mercy hidden in it," we have found the essential goodness of life even in the darkest of corners. Rumi teaches: "The highs are hidden in the lows. Spring is immanent in Autumn. Don't run away from anything."

When we complain about the suffering in our lives it is often because we do not understand that what is happening is actually for our benefit. Rumi illustrates his teachings with a story about a sage who saw a snake slip into the mouth of a sleeping man. It was too late to catch the snake, so the sage hit the sleeper hard with a stick. This woke him suddenly and sent him scampering for protection under a tree. The sage picked up a number of fallen rotten apples and stuffed them into the poor man's mouth. "What are you doing to me? What have I ever done to offend you?" cried the man. As he began to curse, the sage beat him with the stick again, shouting, "Run! Run into the wilderness!" Sleepy, confused, stuffed with bad apples and forced to run until he dropped, the poor man's stomach could no longer take it. He vomited and out shot the apples with the snake among them. Seeing it writhing there the man fell down in front of the sage and thanked him. "If I had told you about the snake," said the sage, "you would have been frozen with fear and you wouldn't have had the power to eat the rotten apples or vomit up the snake."

The sage represents the wisdom of the life-process that does whatever is necessary to free us from our ignorance, represented by the snake. When we face death, of course, our suffering is not designed to save our life, but for those with a spiritual understanding physical healing is only one type of healing. There is a deeper healing that does not necessarily prevent death, but rather includes death. The suffering we face at death forces us to vomit up the snake of ignorance, and so facilitate the ultimate healing that is awakening. Kahlil Gibran writes:

Much of your pain is self-chosen.
It is the bitter potion by which the physician within you heals your
    sick self.
Therefore trust the physician, and drink his remedy in silence and
    tranquillity:
For his hand, though heavy and hard, is guided by the tender hand
    of the Unseen.

In the face of the awful intensity of the actual experience of suffering, however, these teachings can sometimes seem inadequate and even trite. But this is precisely the role that suffering plays in the drama of our lives. If it were not for suffering it would be easy to rest content with an intellectual understanding of spirituality, without ever genuinely transforming our state of awareness. It is the very intensity of suffering that makes it such an effective teacher. It compels us to go beyond spiritual ideas and find the reality they represent.

It is easy to be in love with life when the world feels like Heaven, but can we keep our heart open when it turns to Hell? Or do we lose faith in the goodness of existence and retreat into cynicism and bitterness? Do we escape our enforced vulnerability by taking refuge in numb withdrawal? Suffering tests the depths of our present spiritual realization and urges us to further awakening. Suffering shows us that we have not fully transcended identification with the body. It tells us that we have further spiritual work to do. It compels us to let go and reach deeper into the perpetual peace at our center. When life is comfortable there is no imperative to awaken. But when we are touched by suffering we are forced either to run and hide or to transform and transcend.

Suffering can either grind us down or polish us up. Often it is those who have suffered most that end up wisest. They have a depth that those who have had an easier time of things sometimes lack. They exhibit a profound humility, because they know that, at any moment, life can turn their world upside down. They do not trust in the power of their own personality to protect them, because they have experienced firsthand how vulnerable they really are. But through their ordeals they have discovered that there is a deeper power, call it God or the Self, which can sustain them even when they are most broken. They trust the Mystery of Existence to carry them through whatever heartbreak they must face, and this makes them remarkable men and women who inspire others with their irrepressible faith, love, and joy. As Kahlil Gibran writes, "The deeper that sorrow carves into your being, the more joy you can contain."

SUFFERING AND ACCEPTING

The perennial philosophy teaches that by suffering willingly, suffering is conquered. These teachings are particularly well articulated in the Christian tradition and are powerfully represented by the crucifix—a portrayal of a man being tortured in the most awful of ways and yet triumphant over suffering and death. In *The Acts of John*, a Gnostic Christian gospel, Jesus teaches: "If you know how to accept you will be able not to suffer. See through suffering and you will have nonsuffering." If we accept suffering we discover that pain and suffering are not the same thing and so can experience pain without suffering.

I remember, in my twenties, asking for some sort of guidance to help me escape the suffering that was consuming me at that time. I randomly selected a book from a friend's library and let it fall open on a page. My eyes fell immediately upon a line that read: "Suffering is the effort it takes to push away the pain you are feeling." I can no longer remember the title or author of the book, but the insight stayed with me. Suffering is caused not by pain, but by our desire to avoid pain. Pain is a set of unpleasant sensations. Suffering is our refusal to experience them.

Pain comes as part of our karmic curriculum of awakening. Suffering is our response to events that happen to us, caused by our inability to accept experiences that seem to be against our self-interest. What we see as against our self-interest depends on what we think we are. Suffering is the price of believing ourselves to be the body and dedicating ourselves to satisfying its desires and seeking its comfort. The more we identify with the body, the more we suffer. The more we understand our essential nature to be witnessing Consciousness, the less we suffer.

These teachings are undoubtedly confronting. When we suffer most of us feel that we are afflicted by something terrible and out of our control. While not trying to belittle the enormity of suffering, the perennial philosophy suggests that whether pain becomes suffering is actually not out of our control at all. Pain comes to us as part of our karma, but we choose whether we experience this as meaningless suffering or as a challenge and opportunity on the journey of awakening.

The saints and sages are not glorifying pain. Everyone wants to feel good and to avoid pain. We are fortunate enough to live at a time where advances in science have made it possible for us to minimize pain as never before. It would be crazy and inhuman to suggest that we would be better, for spiritual reasons, to stoically bear the worst when it can be avoided. It is part of our collective karma to live in an age when pain control is possible and we should be grateful for that. But whether this necessarily means that we suffer less today than did our ancestors is another matter, because suffering is a psychological rather than physical condition.

Accepting pain as part of our karmic curriculum of awakening requires great courage. Many people find prayer can sustain them in times of adversity. Prayer is a way of communicating with the hidden depths we call God or the Self, which continually cares for us with unconditional kindness. Native Americans encourage spiritual initiates to find a death chant. This is a song or affirmation that can inspire them with strength in times of need. Ultimately, however, the way to endure pain is to become aware of our essential nature, which is always at peace. *The Acts of John* teaches that Jesus is able to endure terrible pain on the cross because he is "a stranger to suffering." Jesus explains "I distinguish the man from my Self." He does not identify with the body in pain, but with Consciousness, which passively witnesses the unfolding drama.

As he approached his death from cancer, Shunryu Suzuki wanted his students to understand that, although he might appear to be in agony, he knew himself to be what he called "Big Mind" or "Buddha," which happened at that moment to be witnessing agony. In this state of being, everything was acceptable. He explained:

If, when I die, the moment I am dying, if I suffer, that is all right you know. This is just suffering Buddha. No confusion in it. Maybe everyone will struggle because of the physical agony, or spiritual agony too. But that is all right. That is not a problem.

MEDITATION 7

Exploring Suffering

The saints and sages teach that suffering is a part of the journey of life. It is not something to be escaped or suppressed, but entered into, understood, and passed beyond. When you are suffering, in whatever way, this simple meditation exercise can help you use the experience as a spiritual practice to nurture your awakening.

Preparation
- Sit or lie quietly in a position you find comfortable. Be relaxed but alert.
- Close your eyes and rest your attention on your breath as it comes and goes. Let your breath settle into a slow and regular pattern as you let go of all agitation.

Meditation
- Pay no attention to your thoughts and focus instead on the feelings you are experiencing in your body.
- If you are experiencing physical pain, become intensely aware of the physical sensations—the throbbing, stabbing, burning sensations, and so on. If you are experiencing emotional pain, become aware of exactly how the emotion is manifesting in your body. Is it a gnawing in your guts or the fluttering of anxiety, and so on?
- Stop pushing the painful feelings away and instead cultivate a state of detached curiosity about what exactly you are experiencing. Investigate rather than react.
- If there is strong mental resistance to opening yourself fully to the bodily sensations you are experiencing, try not to get caught in a battle with yourself, but persevere in gently removing your attention from your mental reactions to your pain and concentrating instead on the physical sensations themselves.
- If focusing exclusively on your painful sensations seems impossible, then

explore your reactions. Watch yourself as you resist your pain. Witness the strength of your desire for things to be other than they are. Simply observing your reactions will distance you from them. As you notice your reactions rather than identifying with them, they will gradually quiet down. When this happens, return to observing the raw sensations you are experiencing.

- Become aware that these sensations, although perhaps intensely unpleasant, are not themselves suffering. Suffering is caused by the futile attempt to push these experiences away. Let these experiences be and they will pass when they have run their course, like a spent storm cloud. Accept the painful feelings and let go of the suffering caused by your resistance to them.

- When you have worked with your suffering as much as you feel able to at the moment, open your eyes.

MEDITATION 8

Letting Go of Who We Think We Are

This meditation exercise uses the imagination to take us, step by step, through the difficult process, which old age and illness can force upon us, of shedding our various ideas about who we are, and so recognizing our essential being as that which remains when all else has been stripped away.

Preparation
- Lie down quietly in a position you find comfortable. Be relaxed but alert.
- Close your eyes and rest your attention on your breath as it comes and goes. Let your breath settle into a slow and regular pattern as you let go of all agitation.

Meditation
- Imagine your body deteriorating through aging or illness, so that you become less active. How does that feel? Are you still you? Who are you?
- Imagine the process of aging or illness making it impossible for you to continue with your work. You are no longer a plumber, teacher, manager, or whatever. Let go of your social identity.
- Imagine you can no longer be economically independent. Let go of your economic identity.
- Imagine you can no longer be an active member of the community. Let go of your need to be valuable to others.
- Imagine you will never drive your car again. Let go of the idea of yourself as a driver.
- Imagine you are no longer able to run when you want to, or take your children out, or accompany friends on a country walk. Let go of the idea of yourself as effortlessly mobile.
- Imagine you can no longer make love. Let go of the idea of yourself as a lover.

- Think of your favorite clothes hanging in the closet and imagine you will never wear them again. Let go of being the stylish person who bought those clothes. It is not you anymore.

- Remember your favorite food and drink and imagine that your stomach can no longer digest these things. Let go of all your familiar bodily pleasures.

- Imagine you can no longer move your bowels and so someone has to give you an enema and wipe your behind. Let go of your pride and social graces. Let go of the idea of yourself as someone who is in control.

- Be aware of the suffering caused by the futile attempt to hang on to the temporary identities that life is forcing you to shed. Let go of the feeling "I must do this" and "I must be that," Stop hurting yourself by holding on.

- Be grateful for all that you have been and let these identities go. Thank your body for all the experiences it has brought you and then let go of everything that pulls you into identification with your physical form.

- Ask yourself "Who am I now that all I thought I was has been peeled away from me? What is left?"

- Let each thought that arises die into the silence. Simply be in the immediacy of the moment. Not this or that. Just being. Nothing to do. Nothing to say. Nothing to achieve. Nowhere to go. No one to go there. Just the empty presence of Consciousness. I AM.

- When you feel ready, open your eyes.

LOVE AND LOSS

Only if one knows the truth of love, which is the real nature of Self, will the strong entangled knot of life be untied. Only if one attains the height of love will liberation be attained. Such is the heart of all religions. The experience of Self is only love—which is seeing only love, hearing only love, feeling only love, tasting only love, and smelling only love, which is bliss.

Ramana Maharshi
Indian sage

The perennial philosophy teaches that death is a necessary juncture in the Cycles of Existence. Yet, even if we have a spiritual understanding of death, losing loved ones can be devastating. No philosophy can compensate us for being deprived of their warm touch, their familiar voice, their reassuring presence, their annoying quirks, their adorable ways. Death inevitably entails loss. At some time in our lives, we are all touched by the finality of bereavement. Death may be a beautiful experience of peace and bliss, but for those left behind bereavement is often a savage and disorientating rupture in the fabric of life. What can the perennial philosophy teach us about loss and grief?

Buddhists tell the story of a young woman whose baby died. This woman, like thousands of others before and since, was overwhelmed with grief. In desperation she carried the little corpse to the feet of the Buddha. He was renowned for working wonders, so she begged him to perform some magic that would help her. The Buddha enveloped her in his loving kindness and replied that he would indeed help her, but that she must first bring him a mustard seed given

to her by someone from a household that had never experienced such a terrible tragedy. The distraught young woman visited every dwelling in her village, but each family only shared with her their own sad stories of loss. She traveled the countryside, going from place to place in search of her mustard seed, until finally she realized she was not going to find a single family untouched by death. Suddenly she realized that death was unavoidable. For the first time she stopped asking, "Why has my baby died? Why is this happening to me?" and instead asked, "What is death? Why do we suffer?" She returned to the Buddha with her new understanding and new questions.

The Buddha welcomed her as a student on the path of awakening and taught her that the suffering caused by bereavement is rooted in our refusal to understand and accept the impermanence of all things. Everything that is born must die. Only the unborn is undying. To transcend suffering, therefore, we must be unattached to the transitory things of life, such as wealth, success, and even our own body and

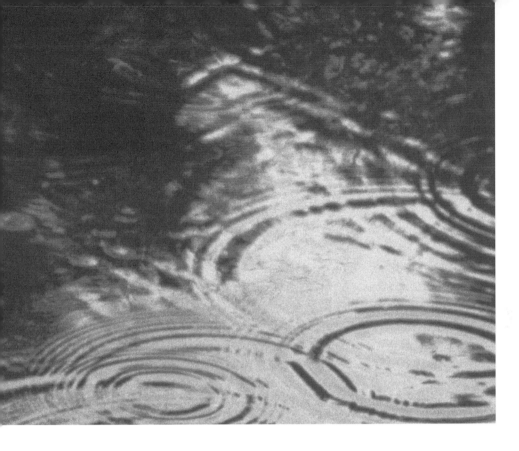

our loved ones. By their very nature all such things must eventually pass away. If we are free from attachments we will accept the comings and goings of life with equanimity. If not we will suffer.

The Buddha is not saying that we *should* be unattached and that failing to be so is some sort of moral sin for which we will be punished by suffering. It is rather that, if we see things as they really are, we will understand that we are already unattached. Attachment is an illusion that arises from misunderstanding ourselves and others as transitory mortal bodies. When we recognize our essential nature, we know there is no need to hold on to anything. All experience is perpetual flux within the eternal permanence of Consciousness.

It is often said that "time is a great healer." Over time we find that people, situations, and things to which we once felt extremely attached no longer have such a powerful hold over us. This is because of our essential detachment. The idea of nonattachment can seem very cold and inhuman, but this is a misunderstanding caused by confusing love with attachment, which the perennial philosophy teaches are quite different. Being unattached is not the same as being indifferent or unloving. Actually it is the complete opposite. True love is nonattachment.

The saints and sages encourage us to be unattached, but they certainly don't want us to stop loving. The perennial philosophy teaches that there is nothing more important than love. Our essential nature is love. To truly love is to enter a holy communion in which we transcend our individuality and partake in that deeper identity in which we are One. Oneness and love are different ways of describing the same Great Mystery, which is our true Self. Love is how Oneness feels. Love is how we experience the paradox of being an individual part of an indivisible Whole. Love is selflessness. The journey of awakening is the process of relinquishing limited self-love and opening the heart to all-embracing Self-love.

The problem is that most of us are not yet aware enough of our essential nature to experience unconditional compassion. Our loving, although real and wonderful, is mixed up with selfish attachment, which is an entirely different thing. Attachment arises because we believe ourselves to be the body and so we hang on to people and things that we believe will meet our selfish needs. Only when we are free of attachments are we liberated from our obsession with our personal self-interest and able to fully express the deep compassion of our true nature. Nonattachment is not unfeeling. It is loving without expecting anything in return. The Chinese sage Confucius writes: "Perfect virtue is compassionate detachment." Compassionate detachment is loving fully and letting go completely. The message of the mystics is love more and cling less.

GOOD GRIEF

When someone we love dies, it is natural to grieve. Grief is not bad. It is the process through which we learn to love and let go. Under the life-transforming impact of loss, grief surges up from the depths of our being, making us really *feel*. If we are not acquainted with such depths of feeling, this can be quite overwhelming, even terrifying. But grief is making us aware of our secret depths, which we have previously ignored. Grief tears open our heart so that we experience just how much love is inside us. It pushes aside the irrelevant trivia of life and shows us what really matters. The intensity of grief brings us right into the present moment. It is the realization that the past has gone and that the future is uncertain. It forces us, like the young woman with the mustard seed, to come face to face with the Mystery of Existence. If we are willing to allow our grief to heal us, its impact can free us to move on, feeling more alive than ever. If we run away from it, it can continue to haunt us in the hidden recesses of the psyche, leaving us crippled and numb.

I had two childhood friends who both lost their father in their early teens and who reacted in very different ways. P spent the next ten years or more obsessed with making sense of death and suffering. He refused to rest content with a superficial understanding of life. He needed an understanding big enough to embrace all the evils of the world, of which his own suffering had made him acutely aware. This sometimes gave him a dark intensity that others of us who had had an easier time of childhood could not understand, but it also forged in him great depth of character, which has made him one of the wisest and most compassionate men I know. G was also a wonderful person, kind, good-natured, and funny, but he took the apparently easier option of suppressing his grief. He turned to alcohol rather than face the pain and confusion, which gradually destroyed him. He died in his thirties when his body could take no more. I have immense love and respect for both of these friends, but I feel their future fate was decided by their willingness or refusal to engage with death and loss when it came calling so early in their lives.

Painful as it undoubtedly is, from the spiritual perspective, grief is a part of our karmic curriculum that offers us the opportunity to become more alive. Attachment, however, turns healthy grief into debilitating despair. It fills us with fear or numbs us with depression. It makes us cling to the past and stops us from healing into the present. What would it be to love and grieve without attachment? How have the great mystics responded to losing a loved one?

When the Taoist master Dong Men Wu lost his son he didn't grieve at all. A friend asked him, "You clearly loved your son very much, why do you not weep?" Dong Men Wu replied, "Many years ago before my son was born I lived without him and was not sad. Why should I be sad now?"

But other great mystics have not shared this emotionless reaction to loss. The Buddhist sage Marpa was engulfed by grief on the death of his son. One of his students asked him, "Why are you so distressed, master, don't you teach that death is an illusion?" "That is true," said Marpa, "and the death of a son is the greatest of all illusions," and he continued to cry. For Marpa, grief was a natural expression of his heartfelt loss, not a sign of spiritual ignorance.

The Taoist sage Chuang Tzu had a different reaction again. When he lost his wife a neighbor went to convey his condolences, but he found Chuang Tzu sitting with his legs sprawled out, pounding on a tub and singing happily. "You lived with her. She brought up your children. You grew old together," said the horrified neighbor. "It is amazing that you are not weeping at her death. To be pounding on a tub and singing—this is going too far!" Chuang Tzu replied, "You're wrong. When she died do you think I didn't grieve like anyone else? But then I looked back to her beginning. Before she was born. Before she had a body. In the midst of the jumble of wonder and mystery a change took place and she had a body and was born. Now there's been another change and she's dead. It's just like the progression of the four seasons—spring, summer, fall, winter. Now she's at rest peacefully in vast Emptiness. If I were to follow after her bawling and sobbing, it would show that I don't understand anything about fate. So I stopped."

89

Dong Men Wu didn't grieve at all. Marpa surrendered himself unreservedly to his grief. Chuang Tzu grieved for a short while and then stopped. The message seems to be that there is no right way to react to bereavement, except to be authentic. To dare to trust our own grieving process.

In recent decades, by contrast, it has become fashionable to believe that grief should follow a certain pattern, which researchers have found is commonly experienced by both the dying and the bereaved. The typical first reaction to bereavement or being diagnosed terminally ill is denial—this is not really happening and if I ignore it, it will go away. The second stage is anger—why is this happening to me, it's not fair. The third stage is bargaining with God—I promise to be a better person if this situation will change. The fourth stage is depression—it is impossible to ever be happy again because everything is meaningless. The last stage is acceptance—I am at peace with the way things are.

We begin by trying to ignore death. Then we try to defiantly push it away. Next we try to negotiate ourselves out of the situation. Finally we become resigned to what is happening. But resignation is not acceptance. Resignation leads to withdrawal and depression. Only when we accept the reality of death can we finally find serenity and equanimity.

The recognition of these stages was a breakthrough in our understanding of the process of death and bereavement. It is often helpful when we are experiencing anger or depression, for example, to know that these are perfectly normal reactions to death. But, although these stages are common, we should not make the mistake of thinking of them as somehow mandatory. I have heard death and bereavement counselors say things such as "I am very worried about so and so, he hasn't gone through any anger." Or, "He is not grieving at all, he must be stuck in denial." These types of comment may be perceptive observations, but not always.

I remember visiting a bereaved young man who was very worried about the fact that he had not cried, which he felt he should. But there are no "shoulds" in grieving. I encouraged him to trust his own grieving process and to cry if he wanted to cry and not to cry if he didn't want to. The relief of knowing he was not "doing it wrong" was all he needed to allow himself to fully grieve in his own way.

A young woman who was a bereavement counselor once told me about visiting her elderly grandfather who had lost his wife. As a compassionate young woman who had been trained to help people "get their feelings out," when she met her grandfather on his doorstep she immediately hugged him and told him that if he wanted to cry and yell that was fine by her. Her grandfather, however, gently extricated himself from her embrace, straightened his back and replied, "Please excuse me, my dear, but my wife has just died." She instantly realized her mistake. She had tried to fit him into her model of grieving, instead of letting him deal with his loss in his way. She was a young woman who believed in crying and yelling about death. He was an old man who preferred quiet dignity. Neither is wrong, they are simply different.

From the spiritual perspective, it is not the form that our grief takes that matters, but our willingness to let it heal and awaken us. The challenge is to accept bereavement as part of our karmic curriculum and willingly enter into the experience. To let ourselves feel whatever it is we feel. To dive into our grief and search out its depths. To welcome the unwelcome guest. This frightening friend.

There is a tendency in our culture to see bereavement as something to cope with and eventually recover from. But from the spiritual perspective, grief is a powerful initiation to be fully experienced, not just managed. The challenge is to grow, not to just cope. Bereavement is not an unfortunate tragedy to get over as soon as possible. It is an awesome life-changing experience, the effects of which must be integrated into our character, so that our love and our loss, and the wisdom we have acquired through the grieving process, become part of us.

The perennial philosophy can't explain away the apparent meaninglessness of loss. The death of a loved one often just doesn't make any sense. Bereavement is not something we can rationalize our way around. The resolution of grief doesn't lie in coming to intellectual terms with what has happened, but in allowing the devastating impact of bereavement to propel us beyond rationality to transrational mystical states of understanding in which we find a faith in the essential goodness of life, which can sustain us through even the deepest sorrow.

From the spiritual perspective the challenge is to transform grasping grief into healing grief. The saints and sages are not encouraging us to withdraw into detached indifference, but to dare to love and let go. To find a love big enough to embrace our joys and sorrows. To love so deeply that we know that, as *The Song of Solomon* assures us, "Love is stronger than death." To understand that, while our loved one has died, our love for them will always be alive. To concentrate on the love rather than the loss. For, as the Christian mystic Meister Eckhart teaches, "Those who suffer for love do not suffer, because all suffering is forgotten."

To free ourselves from selfish attachment into loving detachment is not easy. We need to be patient with ourselves and others when facing bereavement. I remember hearing a Tibetan lama suggest changing the traditional Buddhist prayer "May I not be attached" to the more realistic "May I not be too attached." Unless you are already an enlightened master you are here to learn, which means you will, to some degree, be identified with the body and prone to attachment. That's OK. It's the human predicament. Spirituality is not about giving ourselves a hard time, especially when we are vulnerable. It is about loving, healing, and being real.

The death of a loved one is an experience we would all rather avoid, but when it comes it brings with it the unexpected gift of love, if we are willing to accept it. When my younger cousin unexpectedly committed suicide, I was one of the first people to visit my uncle and aunt, to be with them in their distress. As we sat with the horror and meaninglessness of what had happened, we were more intimately bound together by our shared sorrow and heartache than we had ever been by decades of comfortable family interactions.

I had to cancel the very first death and bereavement retreat I planned to run, because on the day the participants were due to arrive I received a phone call from my mother telling me that my father had had a serious heart attack and was in intensive care, probably about to die. I had been preparing for the retreat by intensively working with my own fear of death and bereavement. Suddenly I was face to face with the real thing.

I had often wondered how I would react to such a phone call. I imagined the panic, the rush to the hospital begging the universe to make everything OK, the desperate last moments, the gut-wrenching loss. It was not like that at all. Probably because I happened to be so well prepared, I found myself sinking into a deep acceptance of the situation and becoming quietly aware of my immense love for my father. Feeling intensely alert and alive, I calmly drove to the hospital, confident in the essential goodness of life and death.

Death was such a big issue for my father that he had been intending to attend my retreat. Yet I found him, lying on a stretcher attached to various machines, serenely waiting to see if he would live or die. I held his hand and we told each other how much we loved one another. In the bittersweet poignancy of the moment, we met in a place beyond words. We came together in a way that transcended our family roles. We were suddenly no longer "Dad" and "Tim," who cared about each other immensely, but who often clashed and argued. We touched as two beings confronting the awesome Mystery of Existence.

And so we remained whenever we met in the days that followed, as we waited to see what would happen. Gradually, however, as it became clear he was going to live, something changed. We started to return to being "Dad" and "Tim." We began to become irritated by each other's idiosyncrasies once again. We stopped just *being* with each other, and reidentified with our roles. Although our relationship has been permanently enriched by the experience, as my father recovered, in many ways we returned to normal.

I am, of course, delighted that my father lived, but I am also grateful for the experience we shared. Confronting his death had made me more myself. It had filled me with faith, not fear. It had taken me deeper into the reality of love. It had woken me up. Ironically, the relief of his recovery had put me back to sleep.

FINISHING BUSINESS

My father and I were lucky enough to be given more time to explore our relationship and to make it clear how much we appreciate each other. Having the awareness that our time with our loved ones is limited is a powerful reminder to resolve our differences while we can. To heal wounds that need to be healed by saying what needs to be said. Many people put up with years of partial communication until it is too late.

From the spiritual perspective life is about learning to love, so it is important to remove any obstacles that stand in the way of our love for each other. The awareness of death can give us the motivation to break through the barriers of fear and inertia that prevent us from opening our hearts. This may involve accepting our differences, asking for forgiveness, or offering forgiveness. All of which often requires great courage.

I remember being moved to tears hearing a grief-stricken gentleman, immediately after his daughter had been blown up by a bomb in Northern Ireland, forgiving the bombers responsible for her death. I felt that I was witnessing true greatness. Here was a bereaved man, with every reason to be bitter and vengeful, letting go into love and in so doing offering the possibility of healing.

I recently heard a middle-aged woman, whose father had also been killed by a bomb when she was younger, relate the story of her reconciliation with the man who planted the bomb, now released from prison. For her this was the culmination of the grieving process that had been working within her for more than fourteen years, leading to healing for her and the man who had touched her life so violently. The bomber told how this remarkable woman's courage had "given him back his humanity" and that he is now working to facilitate other reconciliations between perpetrators and victims in Northern Ireland. This is love in action. The reconciliations necessary in our own lives may be less dramatic, but they still demand all the courage and compassion we possess.

Reconciling ourselves with those who are dying, or if we are dying ourselves, with those we are leaving behind, is often called "finishing business." This is a good phrase because, as Stephen Levine points out, what we really need to do is cease having a business relationship with others and have a relationship of love instead. When we are doing business we keep a tally of what we owe and what we are owed. A business relationship is one in which we hold on to grudges and guilt. On the deepest level, finishing business is more than a settling of accounts. It is transcending this type of relationship altogether and connecting with each other in a deeper way, which makes the settling of accounts irrelevant.

How can we do this? Imagine the tension between two people like a taut piece of string with each person holding tightly to an end. It only takes one person to unilaterally let go for the string to be released. Approaching finishing business as a settling of accounts with someone takes time and great psychological effort, which, when we are dealing with death, are not always available. The quickest way is to simply let go unilaterally into love. For, as Stephen Levine puts it, "The separation and antagonism of a lifetime dissolve in a moment of love."

COMMUNICATING WITH THE DEAD

An awareness of death can give us the impetus we need to "finish business" today, because tomorrow the opportunity may have gone for good. Yet, is it ever really too late for reconciliation? Perhaps it is still possible to communicate with someone in a meaningful way after they have died. Many people feel that they can relate to their departed loved ones in the inner world of the imagination.

I have experienced this myself. Many years ago, when my friend S was dying of AIDS, he deliberately asked mutual friends not to tell me about his illness because he didn't want me to visit him. When last we had met I had been caught up in a somewhat belligerent spiritual mindset, which he had rejected in favor of a wildly hedonistic lifestyle. Since then, things had moved on for me, but he did not know this. As he faced death, he did not want what he feared would be my judgmental presence. This saddened me greatly, but I felt able to reconcile myself with S after his death by imaginatively sharing my love and respect with him, and apologizing for anything I had done in my ignorance to alienate him from me. Is this a real form of communication? That all depends on what we mean by the tricky word "real." For me, it brought a sense of peace that was real, and my intuitive feeling is that, because we are essentially all One, it had effects beyond myself.

Tribal cultures often talk of the dead as still present all around us in some mysterious way. I remember a young girl, at the wake for her dead mother, who pointed to a particularly bright sunbeam and whispered to her baby sister "There, mommy said she'd come back to say goodbye." To me this was a beautifully poetic way of expressing the very real feeling that many people have that, although the dead are gone physically, we can still connect with them in some way on deeper levels.

Many bereaved people continue to sense the presence of their departed loved ones, and feel that they can communicate with them. While writing this book I have been visiting an elderly lady in her nineties, seriously ill with pneumonia, who related to me her experience after the death of her beloved husband, of waking suddenly in the middle of the night to find her room bathed in light and the figure of her husband silently watching over her.

Such stories are remarkably common. A reader of one of my books recently sent me the following inspiring account of his encounter with his dead father:

"In 1995, my father passed away after a long, miserable, and very difficult decline due to Parkinson's Disease. It was a relief, actually, when the end finally arrived. He had been demented and senile for many years—unable to communicate, doped with medications, confined to a wheelchair. The wreckage of a fine man. Caring for him had nearly ruined my mother and had strained our family to breaking point. But on the day he died, at the exact moment that he passed away, I was doing something very, very significant. As the jolting realization of this 'synchronicity' hit me, there was a surge of warmth, an inner glow…and a presence…a demanding, firm, intruding presence. A surge of love and warmth and security and reassurance…and a presence. My father's personality, his affection, his sense of humor…surging within me. Inside my head…and warmth inside my stomach. Warm for the first time in days.

"I called the office to arrange for a couple of days off. I made some excuse to my wife, told her that I needed some time alone for grieving. I grabbed a backpack and some scraps of paper, and went for a long walk in the forest. I walked for hours in a dazed, trancelike blur. The forest and sky seemed filtered by gauze, somehow. A part of my brain (a receptor? something latent, something usually dormant?) seemed to switch on and a dialog commenced. A flood of love and reassurance. My father's humor and his peculiar vocabulary. A query: 'David, my son, ask me questions, ask me now, I can tell you answers, I can send you wisdom and love and guidance—if you will listen. I was trapped inside that sickly devastated body. I couldn't be a father to you, but I am free now. Ask. Ask…'

"So I formed questions—and answers appeared inside my head, instantly. So fast, so quickly—and so truthfully. Answers embedded with wisdom and guidance. 'May I write this down?' I asked. 'Write it all down, David, write as much as you can, David, because afterwards you will be skeptical—that logical, rational, scientific brain of yours won't accept that this is happening. So write it all down—because you will lose your connection, and you will need to reread this material to remind yourself that this connection actually happened.'

So I scribbled…pages and pages…not nearly fast enough…the wisdom and guidance arrived so fast, so instantaneously fast, in response to the questions I formed in my mind. It was exhausting.

"And there was advice about grieving: 'Walk in the forest, David. Build yourself a blazing campfire. Sit by that fire for as long as it takes, and allow yourself to feel…call up these strong emotions and feel them…Feel the emotions, David, my son, who has tried to be so tough and hard and strong for so many years…Feel the emotions, let them flow through you—then throw them into the fire, one by one. Tell yourself, David, I am feeling this sorrow, and this anger—I feel it now—and now I throw it in the fire and watch it burn away into smoke and ashes.'

"At some point I thought/said 'Father, this is wonderful, this is amazing, how can this be happening?' And in reassuring response, 'It was always possible, it will always be possible, if you can focus your thoughts on me. It just takes focus—and clarity. Anger blocks the connection, you must calm yourself, you must dissipate that anger you are carrying around inside you. There is no time or space where I am now. I cannot see you, David, but I can find your thoughts. Your thoughts have energy, David. When you focus your mind, you can send your thoughts outward, and I can find you. I can feel the breeze and see the forest through your thoughts, David. Your thoughts are strong, David. You can do this. You could always do this.'

"The contact gently faded. I was left with exhaustion and amazement and a sense of being loved and watched over. For the first time in a decade I felt loved and protected and secure. A few days later, I walked into the forest and made a campfire and spent most of a day there, quietly crying and sobbing and feeling those emotions—and burning them in the flames. I'm happy to say that this grieving ritual works—for me at least. I have never needed to grieve for my father again."

BEING WITH THE DYING AND BEREAVED

I am often asked "How can we help the dying and bereaved?" The answer is by awakening ourselves—by being what we are: Compassionate Consciousness. Our most important gift is our attention, empty of distraction and full of love. Our spaciousness gives the dying and bereaved the room to fully experience whatever it is they must experience, uninhibited by our reactions.

The more that we have dealt with our own issues about death and bereavement, the more we can be with others in their turmoil without crowding them out with our own confusion. If we have not confronted our own denial and fear, we will simply end up endorsing the denial and fear of the dying and bereaved. If we are unacquainted with the power of our own deep emotions, we will be shocked and disorientated by their powerful emotions. Then we will end up applying what Dr. Elizabeth Kubler-Ross calls "band-aid"—short-term comfort to quell their overwhelming feelings, designed to ameliorate our own distress. If we are aware enough, however, we will be able let go of our own reactiveness and simply be with whatever is happening, and our equanimity and acceptance can then provide a space within which, should they so wish, they can gain some perspective and peace.

It is not what we say or do that counts, but being authentic. If we can honestly acknowledge our human vulnerability, while being sustained by the inner strength of our deeper nature, we can inspire others to do the same. If we can let go of our own fear, or at least honestly own it, we can help others do likewise. If we refrain from smothering others with our personal ideas, we offer them the opportunity to come to their own realizations and resolutions. If we stop pushing the reality of death away, we can be with the dying and bereaved in their agony, when most friends and family have had enough, holding their hand while they go through the horror of their predicament again and again, until they find serene acceptance.

The more familiar we are with simply being the emptiness and unconditional compassion of Consciousness, the more we will be able to be with others in

whatever state we find them, free of judgment and replete with love. Death and bereavement force us to reach beyond intellectual ideas to the reality of love. Only love can transform such suffering into something meaningful, bringing poignancy, togetherness, and courage to warm the chilling futility of pain and despair.

I often recall a courageous lady who came to one of my retreats whose little boy was dying of cancer. He had won a bravery award for resolutely carrying on playing football with his friends, despite having had one of his legs amputated. As a parent myself, I find it almost unbearable to imagine the combination of love, pride, and despair she must have felt. Then, while she was visiting her terminally ill son in hospital, her teenage daughter was killed in a car crash. There was nothing I could possibly say to this lady. No words can address such loss. Yet I was able to be there with her. A loving presence in the middle of the apparent meaninglessness of it all. A silent advocate for acceptance and faith in the Mystery of Existence. Spirituality is about nurturing this state of being in which we commune with each other in compassion. A love big enough to embrace both joy and sorrow.

MEDITATION 9

An Awareness of Impermanence

Islamic scripture recommends, "Be in the world as if you were a stranger or a traveler." In *The Gospel of Thomas* Jesus, likewise, advises "Become a passerby." This walking meditation can help you understand that you are only a temporary visitor to an impermanent world, and that it is impossible to find permanence anywhere but within Consciousness itself.

Preparation
- Take a walk in a graveyard.
- Come into a state of "walking meditation" by relaxing your body and mind and focusing your attention on your breath.

Meditation
- Become aware of the fact that every tombstone marks the memory of a person who lived a life full of joys and sorrows, just like yourself. And that one day there will probably be a similar memorial to your life.
- Become aware that in life we are constantly surrounded by death. Everything around you is impermanent. The people, the plants, the animals, will all pass away.
- Contemplate an old gravestone. See that it is slowly decaying and will eventually crack and disintegrate.
- Contemplate a plant that is growing in the graveyard. See that its death is already inevitable.
- Contemplate yourself and others. We are all visitors passing through life.

- Imagine how this place may look a hundred years hence. What will have passed away and what will remain?
- Imagine how this place may look a thousand years hence. What will have passed away and what will remain?
- If we ignore the reality of impermanence, when death comes calling the shock can be terrible. When we live with an awareness of impermanence we will not be surprised, because we knew this day would inevitably arrive. Contemplate what it means to live with an awareness of impermanence.

MEDITATION 10

Finishing Business

For many of us death is a disturbing prospect, not only because it is the great unknown, but because there is much in our lives left unresolved. Things that need to be said. Wounds that need to be healed. Loved ones left unappreciated. This exercise uses the imagination to help us finish business.

Preparation
- Sit quietly in a position you find comfortable. Be relaxed but alert.
- Close your eyes and rest your attention on your breath as it comes and goes. Let your breath settle into a slow and regular pattern as you let go of all agitation.

Meditation
- Imagine that you are imminently about to die.
- Bring to mind all the people you have known in your life. Is there anything you need to tell someone?
- Have you taken the time lately to let your loved ones know how much you appreciate them? Imagine yourself saying "I love and value you" to your loved ones.
- What enmities and resentments need healing? Imagine yourself working these resentments through.
- What guilt do you need to let go of through seeking forgiveness? Imagine yourself asking for forgiveness.
- What bitterness do you need to relinquish by offering forgiveness? Imagine yourself offering forgiveness.

- Is there anything you need to do to make peace with someone? Imagine yourself doing what needs to be done.

- Imagine yourself "finishing business" with others by ignoring the settling of accounts and unilaterally letting go into love.

- Consider how you can now, wherever possible, actualize in your life these imaginary reconciliations.

BIG MIND

The wise smile at both premature death and excessive old age. They smile, and wish you to smile also, at the changing fortunes of life. For they know that all individual beings are parts of one evolving Whole. Be indifferent to a long life and an early death. Value instead the understanding that all beings form a single universal complex, and that life and death are two aspects of the same Mystery of Existence.

Chuang Tzu
Taoist sage

Underlying the teachings of the perennial philosophy that we have been exploring in this book is an astonishing idea. If we can understand this foundation idea we will be able to understand the whole mystical vision of life and death that arises from it. And if we can do that, then things will never be the same for us again. The idea is this. Everything exists as an expression of One Big Mind. When we finally awaken, the saints and sages tell us, we will discover that the commonsense view of ourselves as separate beings is an illusion. In reality we share the same essential nature. The mysterious presence of Consciousness that is your deeper identity is the same mysterious presence of Consciousness that is my deeper identity. It is the One Consciousness within which everything exists as an appearance. The Big Mind that is dreaming the dream of life. It is God.

We have touched on this idea previously, but I have waited until this last chapter to look at it in more detail, because to do so requires that we dive into the depths of the perennial philosophy, which can be difficult to fathom. I am guessing, however, that if you have come this far with me, you will probably be willing to go the whole distance and get the mystical vision in its completeness, even if that requires exercising mental muscles that most of us seldom use.

In my own experience, I have needed to work with these teachings before I could understand them. Indeed, I am still working with them, and still coming to understand them more fully. Take the time to think these ideas through for yourself. They may seem very abstract at first, because they present such an elevated overview of life. What these teachings offer is a basic intellectual framework with which to understand the nature of existence. Having grasped these ideas, we can more easily directly experience the reality to which they refer in the immediacy of our experience. There is nothing abstract about this. When you get the mystical vision, it could not be less abstract. It is directly seeing things as they are.

THE MYTH OF MANIFESTATION

To help us grasp how and why the One Big Mind appears to be many separate individuals, the saints and sages relate a myth of manifestation. They do not intend us to take it literally, but as an analogy designed to help us picture our predicament. It is a way of approaching the awesome idea that we are One Consciousness identified with many bodies in the process of awakening to our shared essential nature. The myth is this.

In the beginning there was what the Gnostic Christians call the "Dazzling Darkness" and Islamic mystics call the "Dark Light." This is the Clear Light of pure Consciousness, conscious of nothing. And just as if there were light without an object to reflect upon, paradoxically, there would be utter darkness, so Consciousness without anything to be conscious of is, paradoxically, unconscious.

In the beginning Big Mind was unconscious and so unaware of itself. To become conscious it imagined something to be conscious of. The Experiencer appeared to itself as experience. The mystics describe this mythically as God looking in a mirror and seeing Himself as the infinity of all that is. When He does this, however, He believes Himself to be His reflection and identifies with each and every form He appears to be.

And here we are. The One Consciousness of the Universe appearing to itself to be many separate forms. We are all Big Mind mistaking itself for a particular person. The spiritual journey is the process of awakening to our true ineffable identity as the Dazzling Darkness of pure Consciousness. We are the One appearing to be many, undergoing a process of awakening that will reveal that we are One. We are Big Mind becoming conscious of itself. To become enlightened is to recognize that everything is a projection of the Love-Light of Consciousness. Through the enlightened sage, who has transcended the illusion of separateness, Big Mind recognizes itself and the purpose of Existence is fulfilled.

Buddhists compare enlightenment to a drop of water returning to the great ocean of Oneness. I used to find this powerful image a little disturbing, because

it suggested that my unique individuality would be overwhelmed and subsumed,
which doesn't sound very appealing. As I have listened more closely to the saints
and sages, however, I have come to understand that they are not suggesting that
my individuality will be eradicated, but that I will see that it has never really
existed. The end of the illusion of separateness is not a tragic loss of something
real, but the glorious recognition of what truly is. The message of the mystics
is this. There is, and only ever has been, and only ever will be, God playing
hide-and-seek with Himself.

THE CIRCLE OF SELF

To help us understand these teachings pictorially, the ancient Pagans and Christian Gnostics use an image I call "The Circle of Self." Some people find diagrams such as this off-putting, because they seem a bit mathematical, but I have found this simple image extremely valuable. It allows me to picture the relationship between our apparent separateness and our shared essential nature. And it also helps me understand, in a new and revealing way, the cycle of sleeping and waking, the cycle of death and rebirth, and the process of spiritual awakening—and so get the mystical vision more easily.

Imagine a circle with an infinite number of radii extending from the center to an infinite number of points around the circumference. The center represents the Oneness of Consciousness, which extends itself to form the whole circle, representing the contents of Consciousness. The different points on the circumference represent different physical bodies. You and I appear as different bodies on the circumference, but our individual center is *the* universal center. Plotinus explains:

All beings may be thought of as centers uniting at one central center. The centers appear as numerous as the lines starting from them, and yet all those centers constitute a unity. Thus we may liken conscious beings in their diversity to many centers coinciding with one center. They are all One because they share the same center, but appear to be many because of the many radial lines that lead from the center.

The center of the Circle of Self represents our shared essence. Each radial line represents a particular sequence of experiences that is witnessed by Consciousness. The ancient Pagans and Gnostic Christians call this flow of experience "psyche," which is a Greek word usually translated as "soul."

Your individuality is represented by one of the radial lines. It is your psyche or soul. It is all that you experience. That part of the radius within the circle represents your "inner" experience of thinking, dreaming, imagining, and so on. Where the radius meets the circumference represents the densest extremity of your experience—sensation—which is the experience of being a body in the world.

Your particular psyche or soul is what makes you different from me. As the emptiness of pure witnessing Consciousness we have no qualities and so are indistinguishable. What distinguishes us is the different experiences we are having. This is our psyche or soul. We are One Big Mind having different experiences. We are Consciousness witnessing many psyches or souls.

DEATH AND SLEEP

A common inscription on tombstones is "Gone to Sleep." I used to think of this as the ultimate denial of death, but as I have listened to the message of the mystics I have come to understand that "Sleep is the brother of Death," as Rumi puts it. We can use the image of the Circle of Self to understand both the cycle of sleeping and waking, and the cycle of death and rebirth.

Let's first look at the cycle of sleeping and waking. In the waking state, we are aware of the body and the world on the circumference of the Circle of Self. In the dream state we withdraw from the circumference and are no longer aware of the body and the world. We retreat up the radius to deeper levels of our soul or psyche, which we experience as dreams. In the deep sleep state we withdraw completely into the center. We are no longer aware of any experiences at all. We exist in the paradoxical state of being the Dazzling Darkness of pure Consciousness conscious of nothing.

Let's now look at the cycle of death and rebirth. When the body dies we lose awareness of the circumference of the Circle of Self and retreat up the radius into the depths of the psyche, which we experience as afterdeath realms. We then retreat farther toward our deepest identity as Consciousness itself at the center, which we experience as the Clear Light of the Void. If we are spiritually mature enough to recognize this as our own nature we *consciously* merge with the Love-Light. If not we find it impossible to stay conscious and *unconsciously* merge with the Dazzling Darkness, just as we do in deep sleep each night. In the same way that we reappear as the body each morning, we are then reborn.

The sleep/waking cycle and the death/rebirth cycle can both be pictured as the movement of our awareness from the center of the Circle of Self to the circumference and back again. In both cycles we pass through an interim stage of being aware of the deeper psyche or soul, represented by the radius. In the sleep/waking cycle this is experienced as dreams. In the death/rebirth cycle this is experienced as afterlife realms. Each night in the deep sleep state we retreat into the Dazzling Darkness of pure Consciousness at the center and each morning we reappear as a body on the circumference. Death is also a retreat into the Dazzling Darkness of pure Consciousness at the center and rebirth is reemerging as a body on the circumference. The difference being that each morning we reemerge as the same body, but rebirth is reemerging as a different body.

The message of the mystics is this. Death is no more fearful than going to sleep. It is a return to the primal state of Oneness, from which you will return renewed and refreshed, just as you do each morning. Death is the source of life.

THE JOURNEY OF AWAKENING

The image of the Circle of Self can also help us understand the journey of spiritual awakening as the process of progressively extending our awareness from the circumference (body) up the radius (psyche) to the center (Consciousness), and so becoming aware of all that we are.

When we begin the journey of awakening we have only a very superficial awareness of who we are. We think we are the body on the circumference. The first step in awakening to our deeper nature is to "look within" by paying attention to our thoughts, feelings, intentions, imagination, and so on. Gradually we become aware of the depths of the psyche, which we are normally only aware of in dreams.

What happens when we do this? As anyone who has experienced this will know, mundane existence suddenly takes on a dreamlike quality. Life becomes strangely mythic, meaningful, and full of hidden patterns. Synchronicities start happening. We come to see ourselves as spiritual adventurers on a mystical journey. We know there is more to life than meets the eye.

If we look "within" deeply enough we become aware of being the Dazzling Darkness of pure Consciousness, which we normally enter only in deep sleep. Paradoxically, we then discover that what previously seemed to be our inner center turns out to be the spacious emptiness within which everything exists.

Rumi explains: "The bliss of deep sleep is a free sample of the awareness enjoyed by the mystics when they are awake." In deep sleep we experience nothing, but we vaguely remember this state afterwards as a blissful emptiness or Oneness in which we do not exist as a person at all. When we become aware of our essential identity in the waking state, we are consciously aware of this blissful emptiness or Oneness.

For most of us, the bliss of deep sleep is something that dissipates each morning. The enlightened sages, however, never leave the blissful awareness of the emptiness of pure Consciousness, even when they are also aware of appearing to be a body living in the world. They are consciously aware of the mysterious Oneness of the Dazzling Darkness, which we enter unconsciously during deep sleep and at death.

I remember the moment of revelation when it finally dawned on me how simple what the saints and sages are saying really is. The state of awareness that I think of as deep sleep *is* the Oneness of Big Mind. The mysterious source of all. Our shared essential Being. Every night when I go to sleep I dissolve back into the One. The problem is I do this unconsciously. The goal of spiritual awakening is do this consciously, by becoming aware that I am also in the deep sleep state while I am awake, because the Dazzling Darkness is the permanent background of all I experience.

I am aware of the Dazzling Darkness, right now as I write, as an infinite, warm, silent darkness that embraces all that I am experiencing. Because it is outside of my experience, still and quiet, I easily miss this mysterious Presence. I become so enamored of the colors of life, I miss the Dark Light that illuminates them. But when I turn my awareness back on itself I become aware of the emptiness within which the body comes and goes each day when I sleep and wake, and each lifetime when I die and am reborn. The Mystery, of which "Tim" is a manifestation. When I am aware of my ineffable essential nature I have no fear of death, because I know I am dead already. I am always dead, just as I am always in deep sleep. Tim comes and goes. I am. Always and everywhere.

MEDITATION 11

Body, Psyche, Consciousness

This meditation exercise helps you become aware that the states you experience
sequentially as waking, dreaming, and deep sleep are actually happening
concurrently in the waking state. It leads you, step by step, deeper "inside"
yourself, making you aware of the outer world of the body (circumference),
the inner world of the imagination (radius), and, finally, the emptiness of pure
witnessing Consciousness (center), so that you can experience all that you are
simultaneously as One.

Preparation

- Sit quietly in a position you find comfortable. Be relaxed but alert.
- Keep your eyes open. Focus your vision gently on a spot somewhere in front
  of you, but let your awareness be diffuse and ambient rather than concentrated.

Meditation

PART 1

- Become aware of being a body in the world.
- Explore your awareness of the world. What can you see and hear around you?
- Explore your awareness of embodiment. How does your body feel?

PART 2

- Close your eyes and explore the "inner" world of your psyche. What are
  you thinking and feeling?
- Look with your "inner eye" and let images spontaneously appear in your
  imagination. Let yourself daydream for a while.
- Become aware that this experience of the "inner" world of the psyche is the
  state you enter completely when you dream each night.

PART 3

- Now stop paying attention to *what* you are experiencing and concentrate on the fact *that* you are the Experiencer.

- Allow your thoughts to come to a rest. Imagine Consciousness like pure water and thoughts as particles of earth that rise up and make it cloudy when the water is agitated, but slowly settle down when the water is tranquil. Be still and let the mud settle until the water is clear.

- Become aware of pure Consciousness in its pristine clarity and emptiness.

- Become aware that this nothingness is the state of unmanifest Oneness that you enter exclusively in deep sleep, in which you neither exist nor do not exist.

PART 4

- Retain this awareness of pure Consciousness and open your eyes.

- Become aware of yourself as Consciousness that witnesses your inner world of thoughts and the outer world of sensations.

- Become aware that you are simultaneously in the waking state, the dreaming state, and the deep sleep state. The deep sleep state of pure Consciousness is the Dazzling Darkness that illuminates your inner world of the psyche and the outer world of the body.

MEDITATION 12

Living in the Light of Death

This final meditation exercise is a simple practice you can work with at any time, by bringing your awareness to the reality of death and letting it awaken you.

Meditation

- Become aware of the reality of death. Acknowledge the transitory nature of everything.

- See your everyday worries and hassles as insignificant and appreciate life as a precious opportunity to spiritually awaken.

- Let go of the idea of yourself as a separate physical body and become aware of being the Witness of all you experience. Be spacious, unattached, and unreactive.

- Embrace everything within yourself as Consciousness. Be One with all that is. Be Love that unites everyone and everything within its warm embrace.

CONCLUSION

What can anyone know about their end?
There is nothing for it,
but to patiently wait
and see what will happen.

Confucius
Chinese sage

EMBRACING THE MYSTERY

In this book we have been exploring the astonishing picture of life and death offered to us by the saints and sages. Their purpose, however, is not to provide us with reassuring theories to be blindly believed. It is to initiate a process of self-transformation and self-transcendence that will enable us to experience the reality of our immortal shared nature for ourselves. This is a lifetime's—perhaps many lifetimes'—endeavor. But what greater calling could there be than to spiritually awaken? To learn to love fully, live lightly, feel deeply, suffer courageously, and die willingly? To come to know ourselves and, in so doing, discover that there is no need for fear, because life is good and death is safe?

The journey of awakening is not linear. In my experience, it is like the weather. Some days it is all very clear and other days it gets pretty cloudy. But what has gradually changed for me is that I now know the sun is always shining above the clouds of confusion, even when the day is gray. I do not know how it will be when I face death. Perhaps I will be engulfed by an unexpected thunderstorm of raging emotions. Perhaps I will bathe in the clear blue sky of pure Consciousness. What I do know is that my own journey has taught me to trust the process of awakening. To appreciate its gifts of grace and accept its challenges.

Have the teachings of the perennial philosophy helped me overcome my fear of death? Like many people I find ideas such as reincarnation and the existence of an afterlife reassuring, but for me they remain only inspiring speculation. Until I experience their reality, they remain only theories, albeit propounded by those I have come to respect. Even if I took these ideas on trust, they are so vague that I would still have no idea what experiences my particular karmic curriculum would prescribe for me. What I do know is that the saints and sages have helped me glimpse the awesome reality that I am Being itself and so will always continue to Be. These glimpses of my deeper nature have been about transformation rather than information. I have not intellectually understood any more about life and death than I did before. Rather I have found myself communing with an all-embracing Love and an all-subsuming Oneness. Self-knowledge is not like intellectual knowledge. It is a direct apprehension of the Mystery of Existence.

After all my explorations, death remains an enigma. The mysterious nature of death reminds me of the mysterious nature of life. For me, the perennial philosophy gives meaning to life and death, and inspires me with the confidence to transcend ideas and embrace the Mystery. We think death is frightening because it is the unknown. But it is what we are convinced we do know, rather than what we don't know, that makes death frightening. When we think we know that we are the mortal physical body death is terrifying. If we let go of this idea, death is just a mysterious event at the conclusion of the utterly mysterious process we call life.

The Pagan sage Heraclitus writes "Human beings can't begin to conceive what awaits them at death." I do not know what death is, but as I have awakened I have found that it no longer overwhelms me with fear of the unfamiliar, but with wonder at the miracle of the Mystery. I have been surprised to be filled by a profound faith, beyond the scope of words to ever really express, that all is well. That life and death are necessary parts of the process through which the purpose of Existence is being fulfilled. I have found the quiet confidence that Walt Whitman is right. "To die is different from what one supposes. And luckier."

To One Shortly to Die

From all the rest I single out you, having a message for you,
You are to die—let others tell you what they please, I cannot
  prevaricate,
I am exact and merciless, but I love you—there is no escape for
  you.

Softly I lay my right hand upon you, you just feel it:
I do not argue, I bend my head close and half envelop it,
I sit quietly by, I remain faithful,
I am more than nurse, more than parent, more than neighbor,
I absolve you from all except yourself spiritual bodily, that is
  eternal, you yourself will surely escape,
The corpse you will leave will be but excrementitious.

The sun bursts through in un-looked-for directions,
Strong thoughts fill you, and confidence, you smile,
You forget you are sick, as I forget you are sick,
You do not see the medicines, you do not mind the weeping
  friends, I am with you,
I exclude others from you, there is nothing to be commiserated,
I do not commiserate, I congratulate you.

Walt Whitman

FURTHER INFORMATION

For more information on the author, his books, lectures, and seminars visit his website: www.timfreke.demon.co.uk

Books by Timothy Freke include:

Tao Book and Card Pack Godsfield Press (UK), Sterling (US)

The Heart of Islam: Inspirational Book and Card Pack Godsfield Press (UK), Barron's (US)

Rumi Wisdom: Daily teachings from the great Sufi master Godsfield Press (UK), Sterling (US)

Encyclopedia of Spirituality: Spiritual inspiration to transform your life Godsfield Press (UK), **Spiritual Traditions**, Sterling (US)

The Jesus Mysteries: Was the "original Jesus" a Pagan God? co-author Peter Gandy, Thorsons (UK), Harmony (US)

Jesus and the Goddess: The secret teachings of the original Christians co-author Peter Gandy, Thorsons (UK), **Jesus and the Lost Goddess,** Harmony (US)

Hermetica: The lost wisdom of the pharaohs co-author Peter Gandy, Piatkus Books

Lao Tzu's Tao Te Ching: A new version Piatkus Books

Life's Daily Meditations Sterling (US)

Shamanic Wisdomkeepers: Shamanism in the modern world Godsfield Press (UK), Sterling (US)

Taoist Wisdom: Daily teachings from the Taoist sages Godsfield Press (UK), Sterling (US)

The Principles of Native American Spirituality co-author Wa'Na'Nee'Che', Thorsons

Zen Koan Card Pack: A new way to enhance your life through the wisdom of Zen Stewart Tabori Chang (US)

Zen Wisdom: Daily teachings from the Zen masters Godsfield Press (UK), Sterling (US)

PICTURE CREDITS & ACKNOWLEDGMENTS

A big thank you to Debbie Thorpe of Godsfield Press for encouraging me to write this book and to all who have helped bring it into being and make it look so beautiful, especially Mark Truman, Lizzy Gray, and Joanne Jessop for editorial work; Lisa McCormick and Emily Wilkinson for design; and Vanessa Fletcher for picture research.

CORBIS: pp. 2 FK Photo, 11 Richard Cummins, 20 Scott Faulkner, 36 D. Boone, 47 Ed Wargin, 49 David Muench, 57 James L. Amos, 80 Jon Sparks, 90 Robert Landau, 95 Adam Woolfitt, 101 Geoffrey Taunton/Cordaiy Photo Library, 102 Richard Cummins, 109 James Randklen, 111 Tom Bean, 122 W. Cody, 124 Stuart Westmorland. GETTY IMAGES: pp. 37 Stone/Chris Sanders, 41 Telegraph Colour Library/Bavaria, 83 The Image Bank/Pal Hermensen. NASA: p. 18

INDEX

INDEX